To Griffin!

31
DATES
IN 31 DAYS

Tamara Duricka Johnson

SEAL PRESS

31 DATES IN 31 DAYS

Published by
Seal Press
A Member of the Perseus Books Group
1700 Fourth Street
Berkeley, California

Library of Congress Cataloging-in-Publication Data

Johnson, Tamara Duricka, 1977-
  31 dates in 31 days / Tamara Duricka Johnson.
    p. cm.
  ISBN 978-1-58005-366-2
  1. Dating (Social customs) 2. Mate selection. 3. Man-woman relationships. I. Title. II. Title: Thirty-one dates in thirty-one days.
  HQ801.J645 2011
  306.73092--dc23
  [B]
                                    2011025320

10 9 8 7 6 5 4 3 2 1

Cover design by Gerilyn Attebery
Interior design by Tabitha Lahr
Printed in the United States of America
Distributed by Publishers Group West

For my loving husband.

In memory of Watson.

Some of the names have been changed, but the dates, events, and embarrassing moments are all real.

CONTENTS

THE CATALYST

I'm retiring from relationships. Given my dating track record, it seems the only reasonable route to go. What, you might ask, was the catalyst for making such an extreme decision as getting an AARP card for singles? I'll tell you.

It was the summer of 2008. I sat with my boyfriend in a crowded subway train, exhausted from another long day in New York City. I had spent the day with him, trying to have fun and rekindle the love we had rushed into six months earlier. But even in the midst of it, I knew my efforts were fruitless, too forced. As we headed uptown toward my apartment in Harlem, he sat with his shoulders folded into his chest and his hands tucked together between his knees to avoid any physical contact with me. He seemed robotic, with no emotion, and his silence was coated with an edgy energy. His body language only made the memories of his once-loving embraces all the more painful.

How did I trap myself into yet another relationship of ups and downs?

I have always been willing to make sacrifices for my relationships, but given how far adrift we were from each other, I figured I'd have to offer some pretty dramatic ideas to shift us back into "love mode."

I opened my mouth, debating my carefully calculated words. They came out slowly.

"What . . . can I . . . do *differently* . . . to make it easier for you to communicate with me?"

He turned his head, looked at me blankly, and shrugged. "I think I'm just done."

I swallowed the gasp I felt creeping up my throat. I looked around at the other people on the train, who seemed preoccupied with their own thoughts. *Did they just hear me get DUMPED?*

I turned to my all-too-suddenly-ex-boyfriend and desperately offered suggestions, grasping to make the relationship work. *Maybe we just needed a break? Maybe I could be more patient and understanding? Maybe we could find some more activities or search for more common interests? Anything!*

He was unresponsive and uninterested. Done with our relationship and the conversation.

I was heartbroken. And humiliated. I wondered how our whirlwind relationship could have peaked and crashed so suddenly.

For the next twenty stops, my head swirled with confused, hurt, even angry thoughts. Angry at myself for acting so desperate, angry at him for being so insensitive.

I couldn't help but wonder what the short, tubby businessman standing next to me was thinking. He must have heard me all but begging my man to stay. Did he think I was pathetic? Or worse—*was* I pathetic? Why did I even care what he thought? Consider what I was wrestling with: I was thirty years old. I was a successful network television news writer. I had an Ivy League graduate degree. On paper, I was a catch! Never mind that I couldn't cook and always ate takeout, that I lived alone with a cat—and a dog—that I worked too hard and behind the scenes, or that I had never thought of myself as one of the pretty girls. All things considered, society pretty much expected me to be married by now. Worse, *I* expected it. *Hey, businessman,* I felt like saying, *I am somebody. I have dreams. I want to be loved and give love. And I think I could be a really great girlfriend! You should have seen the work I put into this relationship. You should have seen what kind of spark I had at the beginning . . .*

I had fallen for my ex quickly. He was a tall, blue-eyed blond who was smart, attractive, and successful. Even though he lacked the communication and compassion I so desperately craved in a long-term partner, I liked him. My friends dubbed him Boring Guy because of his silence at parties and his general unwillingness to step outside and have fun around the city. Instead, he usually opted to sit on the couch, avoid talking, and observe the rest of us enjoying ourselves as we bantered about nothing and everything.

So what was it about him? Well, for one, I thought he was beautiful. He spoke with eloquence, like no man I had ever met, enunciating his every word and properly punctuating his points. He would whisper the "h" in words like "what" and "where," which made him appear even more brilliant and composed when he uttered simple phrases like, "Why, thank you." I thought such handsome characters appeared only in Jane Austen novels. I felt lucky to have my very own Mr. Darcy.

I believed that under that eloquent facade, he had an equally eloquent heart. Did I mention that I'm an optimist?

We started dating in January, just as I was moving into my apartment in Harlem. I thought of my new home as a sanctuary, a big empty space where my dog could run around, which I would one day furnish when I'd save up enough money, and where I would have lively dinner parties. I painted my living room in bright, rich colors with names like Dragon's Fire, Dandelion, and Safron Sunset. I stenciled the word "JOY!" in a vibrant marigold, reminding me of my own blissful pursuit of happiness and the blooming love I felt in my heart.

I suppose—in some way—when I began dating Mr. Beautiful but Boring, I knew in my gut that our relationship would end some day. But it was 2008, and I'd been dating since New Kids on the Block were together—the *first* time around. I was ready to stop dating and find a man to share my happily ever after with. Like a lot of women, I felt thirty would be the perfect year to find some dreamy guy and get married. I thought Boring Guy was a good possibility. What if he could *become* my dream guy?

A muffled voice announced our subway stop from the speaker overhead: 125th Street. The doors opened and I pushed my way into the stinky gray subway station and what, at that moment, felt like a dismal, lonely future.

I tried to keep my pride and grace intact as we walked up the stairs to street level. "Well," I said, as confidently as I could, "I suppose this is the time I say thank you and goodbye."

He reached out and gave me a hesitant hug. It was rigid, polite—unfeeling. And then he left me.

My heart hurt as I felt that familiar hole of loneliness set in. He followed a long line of men, including five near-engagements, all relationships I felt were my failure rather than theirs. I turned toward home, feeling defeated and fatalistic. "I'm never gonna get married," I mumbled.

I stopped in the middle of the sidewalk, suddenly panicked. For me, it had been simply a given that I would one day marry and make a family of my own. It was the next step in my life plan. Period. So was this sudden revelation true? Was I really destined to be a singleton the rest of my life? Would I never settle down with someone I could just be myself with? Why didn't Boring Guy love me? What was I doing *wrong*? Why did I keep investing so quickly in men I wasn't sure about? And why did I make that mistake over and over again?

When I reached my apartment, I opened the door and was greeted by enthusiastic, friendly barking. *At least somebody loves me!* My dog, Watson, his tail wagging with happiness, followed me to the couch where I promptly curled into a ball and cried.

For a few weeks.

Boring Guy was my second breakup within a year, and what felt like the millionth breakup in my lifetime. I'd become accustomed to sitting pitifully on the couch, listening to sad songs on repeat, and wishing for apologetic phone calls. When I was in college, my boyfriend broke up with me the day before I had my wisdom teeth removed. I writhed in pain—from my heart, my gums—for two weeks. I called the psychic hotlines for comfort, spending $200 in hopes someone would predict our reconciliation. When my pain medication wore off, I made the obligatory drive by his house, leaving a note that read: "Just stopped by to say hi." He lived two hours away.

For as long as I could remember, I had been jumping into relationships too quickly, only to feel regret just a few months later. I had developed a habit of investing too much too soon, sharing my secrets early on, professing my love after only a few weeks, only to wonder a few months later, *Do I even* like *this guy?*

In over fifteen years, my dating habits not only lacked improvement but had become *worse*. I started wishing I could just magically get dating out of the way. I wanted relationships to be simplified. Couldn't I just skip all of the flirting, the uncertainty about whether he liked me, the anticipation of hoped-for phone calls, the pain from potential and eventual breakups? Couldn't we just immediately identify as a match—or not? Couldn't we just go from *meet* to *mate?*

It was time to stop feeling sorry for myself. I had to peel myself off the couch, get out of my pajamas, take a shower, and turn my life around.

I turned on the faucet and stepped into the tub. *Why do I always end up thinking about all the lessons I have learned* after *my relationships end? Couldn't I just learn all those lessons along the way?*

And then it slowly started to make sense. What if I stopped looking at relationships as a means to an end? What if I stopped worrying about finding someone to end up with and instead just focused on what I was learning and who I was becoming along the way? What if I could just *date?*

I felt an unexpected power come over me. I needed to start all over, go back to the very basics of dating. I would re-learn the fundamentals, beginning with first dates. I decided to give up every dating habit I had. I would quit diving into relationships with men and would instead start investing in a healthy relationship with myself. I would toss aside the lists I had made of my "ideal guy." I would stop wondering if every guy I saw on the street was The One. I would throw out the net and be open to dating guys I never would have thought to date before. I would be open-minded and positive. And I would hope to learn something from every date. I would give men a chance. And I would give myself a chance, too.

I hopped out of the shower with excitement. I traded in my pajama bottoms for a new pair of jeans and got to work. I called my girlfriends, announcing my newfound commitment to life, instead of a life geared toward finding commitment. When it came to dating, I would allow myself to go out only on first dates. I would beg the universe to help lure good men into my life, and I would avoid gaining another boyfriend too quickly. I would finish up the year by focusing on JUST DATING.

A few months after my resurrection from the couch, I celebrated my December birthday by taking my dating declaration to an entirely new level. I would kick off age thirty-one by embarking the ultimate dating challenge.

THE PLAN

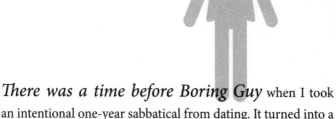

There was a time before Boring Guy when I took an intentional one-year sabbatical from dating. It turned into a three-year drought.

Lots of questions come up when you're not dating anyone. *Are you unhappy you're alone? Have you tried online dating? Aren't you worried about your clock ticking?* And some people start to wonder about your sexuality. Including your mother.

"Ya know," my mom said to me, "if you're interested in women, I'm completely supportive."

I did a mental double take. "What was that?" I asked, flabbergasted.

She spoke carefully, just in case I hadn't heard her. "I'm okay if you're attracted to *women*."

I sat in a moment of silence, digesting her assumption, trying not to laugh. "Mom . . ."

"Yes?" she said expectantly.

"I'm not a lesbian."

I looked at her, expecting relief. Did I see *disappoint-ment?*

"I'm just saying that it's okay if you are," she stumbled. "It's just that . . . I know *so* many more likable women than I do men."

"Mom . . . I'm not gay. I'm just single."

This was not the sort of conversation I was expecting, and the odd disappointment in her silence was a little disconcerting. Maybe she thought this would be the easiest fix. But really, in all the scenarios I could imagine that could cause my mother disappointment—dropping out of college, getting arrested, becoming a drug addict—I never once considered that being *heterosexual* would be a disappointment. And what did being single have to do with sexuality, anyway? Didn't gay women go through dry spells, too?

"Ummm, I'm . . . *sorry* I'm not gay . . . ?"

Mom didn't look convinced.

Months passed without a hint of a date. I invested my time in my work, my friends, my family. I seemed to have the perfect life of solitude: a solid job, a great little home, a great neighborhood. It seemed ideal. Just add husband and stir.

And then I started to feel a little lonely. I wanted someone to be by my side. I wanted to share my time and thoughts. I wanted to give love freely. I wanted to feel love in return. I wanted a best friend.

So I got a dog.

I went to the Humane Society, and there was Watson, staring longingly at me with his rheumy beagle eyes—looking for rescue. He was everything a single gal could want in a partner: He was vulnerable, abandoned, grown-up, handsome, and hungry, and he was looking for someone to love unconditionally. He was perfect.

I took him home and quickly learned he was like the many men who came and went in my life: Simply put, he was more than I could handle. He was demanding of my time, food, and energy. My life was controlled by his crap. He was a rascal. My friends talked about him behind my back, saying he wasn't good enough for me. But I ignored their criticisms. He was there for me when I felt lonely. He was there when I wanted someone to play with, to take on walks, to be silly around.

Boring Guy couldn't stand him. Watson looked sternly into the blond's eyes and growled, sensing something I didn't. Maybe Watson knew that my handsome suitor wasn't meant to be a longtime lover. When we broke up, Watson was there, with his big droopy brown eyes, to comfort me as I mended my wounded heart. He would lie by my side at night and be my pillow as I slept. He was there as I readjusted my attitude and felt empowered, rather than depressed, by my new single status. And then, just days before my thirty-first birthday, he left me.

I remember crying wildly as I brought him to the veterinary hospital. Why was this happening? Why now? Why him? "Watson," I said, "I don't want you to leave me. But I promise you that I won't be selfish if this is your time to go." He was my best friend. Within a few hours, he was gone.

My birthday arrived days later, accompanied by a cake—its candles, my friends, trying to warm my soul. My girlfriends stood by my side as I cried, wishing for a fresh start.

"I thought I hit rock bottom weeks ago," I said, "but now I feel even more alone than I did before."

My friend Rachel, who was never at a loss for unsolicited wisdom during heavy moments, quipped, "Rock bottom has a sneaky way of taking you as close to death as possible." She paused for effect. "And then there's a trap door that opens, soaring you straight to Hell."

Nothing like an upbeat perspective. I loved her for it.

In place of Watson, my girlfriends came to my aid. For several days we sat on the floor in the living room, watching romantic comedies and eating high-carb food and ice cream. Amy, my business-savvy computer whiz of a friend, scanned her laptop, popping back and forth between her web design business and her online search for smart, available men. Rachel pored through my closet, pulling out flirty outfits.

"No more pajamas for you," she insisted, with a tsk-tsk wave of her finger. "I know you feel like crap, but there's no reason you can't look hot in the meantime. Weren't you just saying you felt 'empowered' by your singledom? Well, let's get to it."

She was a bossy and wise diva. My own personal Liza Minnelli, on a mission to get me back in gear.

"Whatever happened to your idea about focusing on 'just dating'? Can't we hook you up for your birthday?"

"Rachel," I moaned, "I have no idea what I was thinking. How would I find guys to go out with anyway? And I'm *awful* when it comes to first dates. Remember?"

The last first date I'd had after Boring Guy was ruined just as the guy arrived. Watson bolted out the front door, I chased after him, and my door shut behind me, locking all of us outside the apartment. My date and I scaled the wall of my building and crawled through my bedroom window. No second date on that one.

And then there was the time at the end of a perfectly nice dinner when I discovered that someone had stolen my purse from underneath my chair. I thought I handled the rest of the evening with my date, the police officer, and the theft report with grace. I was surprised when I didn't get a second date with him, either.

One of my worst dates, however, was my very first "first date" in high school, when an upperclassman took me to watch one of our high school football games. He brought me home early, hugged me goodbye, and drove home with one of my best friends, who promptly lost her virginity to him.

Rachel rolled her eyes as I reminisced. She'd heard these stories before. She'd *lived* similar stories before. She ignored me, digging around in my jewelry box instead, until she found a pair of earrings to match the animal-print top she'd pulled out. She held them up against me, admiring her selection. "Will you stop hating on yourself? You're amazing and fabulous. This self-loathing needs to stop. Why don't you go out on a bunch of dates this year? Screw being thirty. Make *thirty-one* your year."

Without lifting her eyes from her computer, Amy offered an idea. "Why don't you just spend your next year going out on thirty-one dates?"

My friend Amy is a genius.

I could slap myself out of self-pity by immersing myself in a new dating project. It would be part distraction from my empty life, and part lesson in how to live and love again. Maybe it would help me get over my broken heart. Maybe it would even somehow help me get over men in general. I would give it my all. And hopefully, I would learn something. Desperation can be a great motivator.

Amy's suggestion became the basis of a major plan. I would develop a one-month master's course on men. I would start by throwing out my bad dating habits and old criticisms: I would not see every date as a future husband. I would not judge a man instantly on whether he lived up to that standard. I would not shortchange my own potential to learn and have fun for the sake of fun itself, not the promise of finding The One. I would immerse myself in the dating world, going out with one man every day, remaining a positive and open-minded student, hoping to see what each one could teach me.

I would start from scratch.

But that wasn't all. I'd commit to sharing my dating experiment with others.

Amy used her computer prowess to help me develop a website where I would write about each of the dates, and the lessons I learned along the way.

I came up with a set of rules, or constants, that would give my project the parameters of a good social experiment. With New York City's female-to-male ratio of 5:1, I knew it could be tough to find guys to go out with, so I came up with a few gimmicks, hoping to convince potential dates that my project would be worth their time.

THE RULES

- ☑ Each date will cost less than $31
- ☑ Each date must last at *least* 31 minutes
- ☑ Dates will take place in a public setting
- ☑ No drugs
- ☑ No alcohol (Yes, seriously. None.)
- ☑ No married men
- ☑ Some of the dates will be with friends
- ☑ Some dates will be with strangers
- ☑ Some will be setups
- ☑ Date No. 31 (Valentine's Day) will be a second date

I would offer to pay for the dates. After all, if I were looking at the experience as a true "master's class," I could pay tuition. I put a price cap on each date to make it possible for my budget: $31.

Fearing boredom and a growing waistline, I decided to eschew typical dinner dates. Instead, I took advantage of living in one of the world's most culturally rich cities and wrote up a long list of all the sites I still hoped to see. If I didn't end up enjoying the company, at least I could enjoy the activity.

I also came up with a list of ground rules that made me feel comfortable in the presence of strangers, keeping my dates safe, sober, and sex-free: All dates must be in public places, free of alcohol, and be with unmarried men. Plus, I had my own little secret boundary for myself: No kissing. I'd seen enough reality television to know that I didn't want to be the girl who spends all her time making out with her dates instead of getting to know them. I didn't want kissing to get in the way of the learning process—even if it ended up being excruciating to resist.

I went to an office supply store and printed a bunch of business cards, simple ones that read: "31datesin31days.com." They would serve as conversation starters or would be my last-ditch effort to engage a cute guy I would never have the nerve to approach. The project started to feel legitimate—and extremely intimidating.

Finally, I added a little twist to the end of the project. While the first thirty dates would all be first dates, number thirty-one would be special: It would be a second date with one of the first thirty guys. My online readers would vote for their favorite guy and help me pick "Date 31." And *that* date would fall on a special Saturday—Valentine's Day.

♥

I outlined the whole project, but I still needed to jump what seemed like the biggest hurdle—getting thirty guys to go out with me. I doubted whether everything would come together and wondered if I was just setting myself up to look like an idiot. I shared my fears with my girlfriends—*Maybe this isn't a good idea. Maybe I shouldn't do this. This is quite clearly the dumbest thing I've come up with in my life*—and they, being the wonderful friends they are, showed me their unwavering support.

"Stop hating yourself and just do it," scolded Rachel. "It'll turn out great. I guarantee you won't regret it."

"Great. *You* get to help me fill my calendar, then."

And so the project began. In the middle of January 2009. I would face the ultimate dating challenge of my life . . . with only three dates lined up.

THE LIST

A few years ago, long before Boring Guy served as the unwitting catalyst to the dating project I'm about to embark on, I enlisted the help of relationship coach Val Baldwin. She's a blond mom with a big house and a great manicure. She joyfully bills herself as "Val the Relationship Gal." She's cute, bubbly, and still madly in love with and married to her high school sweetheart. She's a grown-up cheerleader: a life and love coach who fuels her energetic personality by helping others get their lives in gear.

When I arrived at her home just outside Portland, Oregon, she welcomed me with a bright smile and open arms. "Tamara!" she beamed. "Come *in!*"

I couldn't help but hug her. Her warm energy was infectious.

She led me into her huge home office with high ceilings, rich chocolate-colored walls, and classic Ethan Allen–style furniture. I wiggled my way into one of the comfy leather chairs.

Val sat tall across from me and got down to business. She looked at me with bright, excited eyes. "So, Tamara. Tell me the kind of guy you're looking for."

Here was the million-dollar question, the reason I'd gone to see her. I was in search of Mr. Right, and in my haste to find him, I kept settling for Mr. Right Now. I hoped by sharing my ideal with Val, she'd help me figure out where I'd been going wrong.

I hedged around my list of qualities: a nice, funny guy who wanted a family, wanted to spend lots of time with me, and shared similar interests. Spoken aloud, my answers sounded suddenly generic, ones that would be acceptable for anybody searching for love.

She shook her head. "Tamara," she chided, "we need to get you to focus a little better on the kind of man who would fit with *you*." She pulled out a sheet with a list of more than a hundred adjectives and said, "These are just some suggestions to get you started. I want you to try and narrow down a list of ten requirements you need in a man."

"Requirements? You mean like, deal breakers? Red flags?" I nodded my head in agreement, "Yeah, I'm well aware of *those!*" I quickly thought back to the list of deal breakers I'd been creating since college: no high-tenor voices, no unicyclists, must like sushi . . . Maybe I was overthinking this.

"Deal breakers," Val explained, "are *similar*. What I'm talking about are 'requirements.' What specific characteristics do you need in a man to make your relationship work? These are your 'nonnegotiables.' I'm not talking about the *extras*, like 'plays the guitar' or 'loves to ski.' These requirements are not *wants*, they are *must-haves*. What I'm talking about are those very essential basics. Think of it this way: If these qualities were missing, your relationship would *not survive.*"

I stared at her long sheet of suggested character traits. It would be hard to narrow my list down to ten. I started to lose faith in the concept. I could just hear the echoes in my head from friends who already claimed I was being "too picky" or the others who claimed I was "not picky enough." But I figured my own attempts weren't working in my love life, so it was time I tried someone else's tactics. I took Val's advice.

Over the next two weeks she helped me narrow my list down to ten. I was excited to see all of the qualities of my own "Mr. Perfect" on paper. *Finally,* I thought, *I know what I want!*

I wrote the ten requirements down on sticky notes and stuck them everywhere: on my mirror and my computer screen, in my journal, on the fridge. Then I sent an email to some friends:

Dear friends,

Recently I made a list of qualities that I would like in my husband. If you meet anyone who has these qualities, please don't hesitate to send him my way! Here is my list (in no particular order—they're all important!):

- Mutual emotional support
- Mutual physical attraction
- Intellectual equal
- Independence

- Driven
- Shared sense of humor
- Shared religious beliefs
- Common vision of life
- Effective communication
- Family oriented

I pressed "send" and hoped the universe would send The One my way. Maybe Mr. Everything-on-the-List was just waiting to pop miraculously into my inbox while angels chanted the "Hallelujah" chorus.

That was six years, two jobs, one state, and a dozen guys ago. Since then, most men I had dated hadn't really matched what I needed but had had other qualities that were appealing to me, like "artsy" or "assertive" or "inspiring." In the end, those relationships led to heartbreak and only helped me add three more qualities to my list of ten core requirements: fidelity, self-awareness, and addiction-free.

I looked at my list time and again, wondering if a man with all those qualities even existed, and if so, would he actually find *me* appealing?

On the days I felt exceptionally critical of myself, I felt cynical, convinced my odds of finding anyone were shrinking. I started wondering if my list might need to be narrowed to more simple requirements, like "pulse" and "penis."

During my recent months of despair on the couch, before my girlfriends intervened, I felt inspired to make yet *another* list. This one outlined a whopping *one hundred* qualities of my "ideal guy." I included all of the qualities I found important—

funny, loves family, loves *me*. I also included bonus character-istics I never actually expected to exist in a real human who could love me: tall, blue eyes, curly dark brown hair, plays the guitar, speaks Spanish, greatest lover ever, likes to cook (since I don't), and is cool enough to be a Boy Scout but not geeky enough to get his Eagle rank. Stuff like that.

I smiled at the unrealistic thought that a fun, complex man like that might actually exist. And then I did what seemed best. I folded up the piece of paper and tucked it away. It was time I started *letting go*. In fact, I set all of my "lists" aside. For years I had held on to my list with pride, as if my awareness of my desires empowered me. But my arrogance wasn't getting me anywhere. I had to put my ego on hold and accept that holding tightly to rigid expectations wasn't the right approach. I was willing to be wrong if that meant I could be happy.

Letting my lists go wasn't easy. In many ways, I felt as if I were giving up on myself. It was kind of like going through my entire wardrobe and giving away all of the skinny jeans I was hoping to someday fit into again. Was I giving up on what I really wanted?

There's a part of me that still hopes someone special will come along over the next month, but I'm accepting that it might not happen. Instead of focusing on finding the right guy, I figure I need to keep my sights on being the right *girl*.

I've sifted through the slew of dating advice I've received over the years, searching for some secret formula I might be missing. I've highlighted and underlined pages in my unusually large personal library of dating rulebooks, which all seem to conflict with one another. One would advise, "Show you're interested!" while the next would say, "Don't call him, ever." I've watched all the dating shows that claim to share the keys to finding love. I've had endless late-night conversations with friends, analyzing our dating lives over fast food and diet drinks. I've even gone to those secret dating seminars where dozens of single women sit on stiff chairs in a cold conference room, feverishly taking notes from one woman writing tips on a dry-erase board. The one major piece of advice I took away? Guys love shiny hair. I tugged at my own tattered blond locks.

I'm screwed.

Some "experts" tell me to wear cute clothes and flip my hair. But others tell me the same advice my mom gave me when I was worried that the kids at school wouldn't like me: "Just be yourself." That comes with its own challenges. What if "being myself" means that all my insecurities are shown? What if "myself" isn't attractive? Or fun? Or interesting? What if "myself" feels bad about who I really am?

It seems like first dates are just ripe with opportunities for all of us to feel bad about ourselves. And here I am, volunteering to have a month of those moments. I feel like I'm about to put myself through a month-long process of job interviews, wondering every day, *"Do you like me?"* and if not, then why?

The only message that seems consistent from the dating gurus—and my mom—that resonates with me is something along the lines of "open your heart and be your authentic self."

I've decided to tuck away the lists and all the pieces of advice and hope for the best. I'll just date whomever I want and will see where it goes. I'll try my best to be authentic. I'll be open-minded. And I'll secretly pray for shiny hair.

DATE 1: ROB

Hey Rob!

My friend Katie passed along your name and email address to me. I'm doing a lil' dating project called "31 dates in 31 days." The premise is simple: For one month, go out every night and do something new with someone new. The challenge here is to keep the price under $31 and we need to survive at least 31 minutes with each other. We critique the date, and I'll blog about it. What do you think? You in?

I'm looking for G-rated dates. Is there anything you haven't done yet around the city that you'd like to check out?

—Tamara (sounds like "camera")

Contemporary art is confusing. I'm looking at a bunch of black plastic combs gathered together into a large sculpture of a man's head, and I have absolutely no understanding of the artist's intent. Pretty much every installation Rob and I see at the Museum of Arts and Design engenders the same quizzical response. But maybe that's the artist's intention to begin with.

I met Rob outside the museum at 6:30 PM. He showed up on time, in a long black trench coat, looking just as I expected him to from Katie's description. He was one of those tough business guys from Long Island whose arms might be too buff for his suit. A tight cut of dark hair, a hole in his ear revealing an old piercing, and a wide strong face. He was holding a pink rose.

I gushed, "Hi Rob!" Seeing him made me even more nervous.

"Tamara?" he asked. He said it slowly, enunciating each syllable. "This is for you." He handed me the rose, shrugging slightly. "I'm not really sure what to do in this case. I've never done this kind of thing before."

"Me neither!" I squeaked, hyperaware that my heart was racing faster than usual, hoping he couldn't hear it pounding in my chest.

He looked surprised by my response. "Really? How many of these dates have you been on?"

"Ohhh," I said, worried that he might be turned off by my answer. "You're my first."

"FIRST? Oh." I couldn't tell by his expression if that was a good thing or not.

Did he think I was an amateur dater? Did he think he'd been schmoozed into something lame that no one else would do?

"So, we're both trying out something new," I said, smiling nervously, hoping that reassured him. I turned quickly to the museum entrance, hoping to avoid having to discuss it further.

He pulled open the door and held it for me as I walked inside the museum. A sign on the admissions counter read: DONATIONS ACCEPTED HERE.

My stomach started to rumble a bit as I reached into my purse. I had already mentioned to him that there was a $31 limit on each of my dates and that I intended to pay for everything. But then all the expert dating tips I'd read crowded my head, one in particular: *A woman should never pay on a first date.* Was that true? Well, so much for tradition. After all, wasn't part of this project aimed at tossing aside convention?

But as I reached for my wallet, Rob beat me to it and paid the $30 admission. He looked at me and shrugged, perhaps uncomfortable with this awkward moment. "Is that okay?" he asked.

"Sure. Yeah, that's fine. *Really.* Thank you," I said, stumbling over myself, feeling unsure whether I'd responded the right way. I intended to pay for each of the dates, but would I have appeared too pushy had I insisted?

I stuffed my wallet back in my purse, and as we waited for the elevator to take us upstairs, I wondered how I might have handled the situation better. *Should I have insisted on paying? Should I have had a conversation about this with him before I pulled out my wallet? Or did he think I was being silly when I grabbed my wallet to pay? Is he one of those guys who think it's too assertive for a woman to pay? Does he want me to just let him be the "guy"?*

It was amazing how much I'd taken for granted with dating before now. I would have always let the guy pay first. But was that etiquette outdated and unfair? I chalked the moment up to experience and made a mental note to see if Date 2 would feel comfortable letting me pay.

The exhibits at the Museum are quintessential New York City. People with wild ideas somehow bring their thoughts to life, and the rest of us look at their grand adventure and wonder what they were thinking. I guess the same was true for me and this project.

I wasn't sure what to think of all the funky contemporary artwork. There was an eight-foot-tall pyramid made of rubber-banded plastic spoons. Another artist had used plastic forks to design a Christmas tree–size lighted lily. And there was a collection of murals of old rock stars crafted from bottle caps.

Rob lingered in front of a free-form wall installation made up of vinyl records and motorcycle parts. He seemed enthralled. I didn't get it.

"Ya know," Rob said to me, pointing at the mishmash on the wall, "I love anything to do with motorcycles."

I nodded, pretending to understand the messy structure that hung before me. "You ride motorcycles?"

"Yep," he said with a prideful smile. "I've got two of 'em."

"*Two?*" I asked. "I've never ridden on one. I think I'd be scared."

"Scared?" he shook his head. "Nah. No need to be. You should come out to Long Island and we can go for a ride sometime. You'd like it."

Come out to Long Island and ride with you? Was Rob already suggesting the possibility that we could have some kind of future? Or was this just a way of making small talk?

I couldn't help but feel myself getting sucked back into my old habit of creating some fantasy future with Rob, imagining myself riding on the back of his motorcycle with the wind whipping through my hair as he revved the engine a little. I would grab his waist more tightly, terrified and excited all at the same time—perfectly willing to put my fate in his hands. He'd yell back to me, "Don't worry! You're safe with me!" and we'd speed down the highway toward our happy, perfect, blissful future.

I shook the wistful thoughts away, making a conscious effort to slip back into reality and act like the cool girl who was willing to try any adventure that scared the living hell out of her. I shrugged. "That sounds like fun."

I don't usually consider myself a risk-taker, but on that first date, I was proving myself wrong. Just a few hours earlier, I had been secretly hoping I would have to cancel my date—and my whole project—because of breaking news. I was wrapping up my work for the day (I'm a segment producer for *Good Morning America*) when we started hearing news that a passenger plane had made an emergency landing in the Hudson River. Everyone on the plane was safe and making their way to land. This story was going to be huge.

But the night shift would take care of the story, so there was no need for me to stay. My coworkers kept giving me the thumbs-up and wishing me luck on my first "first date." I was excited, sure, but I was also scared of putting myself out there for the world to see. What if I could just keep living my life the way I understood it, instead of taking a risk? Then my eye caught Eleanor Roosevelt's famous advice, which I'd posted by my desk to remind myself that this was all about shaking things up:

DO ONE THING EVERY DAY THAT SCARES YOU.

That would be easy. I was *definitely* scared of this project.

By the time the passengers were making their way off Flight 1549, Rob was calling about our final plans. His rich, rumbling voice struck me instantly, sending little shivers up my back. At that point, I knew nothing more than the fact that I'd be perfectly happy listening to him read the back of a cereal box. But then I started getting nervous. Everything started to feel *real*.

As Rob and I walked down the staircase, I couldn't help but wonder about the other people wandering around the museum. Could they tell Rob and I were on a first date? Was my nervousness transparent? Or did I look as laid-back as I was hoping?

"So, Rob," I asked, "what else do you do for fun?"

"Anything outside. This time of year I snowboard. Back in the day, I was actually pretty good. I started out skateboarding. I guess it's just kind of a natural transition."

"You don't skateboard anymore, though?" I asked.

"Nah. Not really. I used to do it all the time," he said, and then in the same casual tone mentioned, "I was actually sponsored for a while."

"You mean, like a professional?"

"Not really. But it was definitely something I did a lot."

"Wow." I shook my head, wondering if I had what it took to date someone who was into extreme sports. "I'm sure I'd be horrible at skateboarding *and* snowboarding. But it sounds like fun."

"Yeah, it is. You've never tried?" he asked.

"Nope." All of a sudden, I realized I couldn't, in fact, picture myself dating this extreme athlete. Didn't we need to share the same common interests? Isn't that important when it comes to dating? Or not? What was I doing, anyway, trying to make a decision about our future so soon?

"So, what about *you?*" he asked. "This project. What's this whole thing about?"

"Well . . ."

I paused, trying to work my way around his question. I was a little hesitant to talk about the project, because I kind of liked feeling as if we were on a real date. For a while, I had forgotten that I had convinced him to go out with me for the sake of an experiment.

"I just wanted to go back to the basics of dating. Just first dates," I admitted. "I feel like I could learn a lot. I dunno. I just decided, why not?" I could feel myself getting shifty. "It's a little crazy, isn't it?" Inside, I was chastising myself. *Why am I seeking validation from him? Isn't this supposed to be about becoming a confident, more independent woman who doesn't need a man's approval?*

"It's daring," he said. "I couldn't do it."

That surprised me, and I suddenly felt more in control of my purpose.

"Whatever, you're Mr. Risk-Taker."

"Yeah, but . . . you've signed yourself up for the extreme sport of dating. And *that* can be risky. Especially in New York City."

He was right. Why was I selling myself short? Maybe I was a wuss when it came to motorcycle rides and sports, but at least I was facing my fear of dating. I was doing something risky. And I was letting New York work its magic.

I clutched my pink rose as we headed toward the door, which swung open with force from the cold wind. I tugged my hat down over my head and wrapped my coat closely against me. "Rob," I said and could feel myself shivering. "Thank you. This was really perfect."

I reached up to give Rob a hug and he leaned down toward me. I wasn't sure if he was trying to kiss me on the mouth or not, and half of me wanted him to, but I turned my head to the side instead and offered him my cheek.

His movement was seamless, and he gave me a quick peck on my cheekbone and pulled me in close for a hug. I embraced him, replaying what had just happened in my head. *Did he just try to kiss me on the mouth? Or am I flattering myself? Am I weird for offering him my cheek?*

He gave me a tight squeeze and I could feel the rumble of his rich voice shake against me. "Goodnight."

Whether I was giddy because of Rob or because of the dates to come, I'm not sure, but I soared on this emotional buzz all the way home. *No pressure,* I told myself. *All fun. And definitely worth the risk.*

All I had to do was get up and try to act cool and do it all over again the next day.

DATE 2: JOEL

Joel always seemed to like me for myself. And that's a relief. After my first-date jitters with Rob, and the pressure of having my inaugural date for this project feel like the equivalent of a blind date followed by a book report, I was looking forward to a more relaxed date with someone I actually knew—and someone I thought I could like.

When I met Joel two years ago, I was dating The Boring Guy. It wasn't until after that breakup that I looked at Joel and wondered, *Hmmm, could I see myself kissing you one day?* He's certainly handsome enough. He's around five-foot-nine, with dark-green eyes that tend to linger and close-cropped blond hair. He's lean but looks fit, and he typically wears just enough scruff on his face to be sexy rather than overwhelming.

He's one of those guys that I can talk to easily about my aspirations, my career, my sensibilities, and my fears without worrying that he's judging me. He's kind and a hard worker. His day job is with computers. At night, he's a classically trained actor who rehearses until late hours.

The whole time I've known him, I've felt a growing romantic attraction to him. I've asked myself on more than one occasion, *Do I like him? Should I like him? Or am I just trying to force myself to like him?* I've been doing my best to maintain our friendship in the midst of my uncertain but growing interest. What I didn't know was whether he was attracted to me. This would be a great opportunity to find out.

Joel was quick to agree to be my second date for the project, and I sensed he did it out of platonic fun. And that he knew he was doing me a favor. He even took the liberty of buying tickets to a dance performance in the Lower East Side.

Great, I thought to myself. *Two for two with guys who won't let me pay.* I was really going to have to work on a better strategy.

But more concerning to me than the issue of he pays/she pays was the fact that among the audience would be a swarm of not only our friends but also Joel's parents.

This would be a first for me. I don't think I ever once asked my parents for permission to go on a date with someone, much less invited them to the occasion.

I sat through the entire dance performance feeling a little on edge, knowing that our friends were watching us. They all knew about my project and seemed to stare at us as if they were analyzing every move. My photographer friend Kat even took a few pictures of us. Would those photos glean evidence of our attraction to one another? Would they reveal my nervousness?

I kept scanning the audience, trying to see if I could pick out Joel's parents. Were they watching me, too? Did they see me looking for them? Would I have to explain my dating project to his *parents?*

Thankfully, we managed to avoid lingering afterward. Joel was happy to be my partner in crime, so we quickly congratulated the dancers in the lobby and slipped past the crowd, making sure we didn't run into his parents. We made a beeline for the coat check, giggling at our subterfuge, and quickly found our parkas.

I slipped on my big black coat and floppy hat and walked out into the frigid night air. "Is it too cold out here for you?" he asked, concerned. We were headed for part two of our night—a stroll across the Brooklyn Bridge.

"I'm okay," I assured him, though I wasn't too sure myself. Across the river, the Watchtower Building flashed the temperature in giant red letters: 8 degrees. I could already feel the tips of my ears hurting from the cold, but I pretended I wasn't freezing—hoping to keep my "cool-girl attitude."

"Tamara," he said, shaking his head at me, "you're *shivering!*"

"I know!" I smiled with teeth chattering. "But I really want to walk the bridge. Maybe the walk will warm me up . . . ?"

He raised an eyebrow, looking at me in hesitant support, like a parent giving in to his determined child, against his better judgment. "Okay. We'll do whatever makes you happy."

As we stepped onto the Brooklyn Bridge, I felt the back of my high-heeled boots slip in between the wooden slats. I focused on each step, looking down at my feet, but what I noticed more was the East River, cold and glassy, hundreds of feet below me. I felt dizzy and my fear of heights kicked in. *Well, great. Now what do I do?* Maybe if I walked on the balls of my feet, I wouldn't have to look down and imagine myself falling through the cracks to my drowning death. *Ha! Take that, acrophobia!* I just hoped Joel wouldn't notice my odd shuffle for the next mile. Maybe my uncontrollable shivering would be a distraction.

"So," I said, trying to keep the focus off me, "tell me about your latest gig. You're in a new play, right?"

"Ah, yes," he announced boldly, "The play!"

Sometimes Joel has a way of talking to me as if he's onstage—proudly pronouncing his words with Shakespearean authority. "It's going quite well. I'm so happy to have work."

"That's great for any actor in the city, right?"

"It is indeed. And what about you? Are you enjoying life?" he asked.

"I really am," I said, glancing at him. "I mean, I have no idea what's in store. This whole dating project will probably take a toll on me. I'm already realizing that it'll take a lot of time to find guys and figure out dates. It's tiring just thinking about it. But I really feel like it'll be worth it in the end. So I'm trying to be positive."

Joel slowed down his pace just a tad, as if he were mulling over his next statement. His voice gentled. "You know," he said, "you're very different from the girl I remember meeting two years ago."

I could feel my eyes growing in shock. "You remember when you first met me?"

"At least I think it was you. Did you have longer hair back then?"

"Ugh. I did," I said shaking my head. "I kept it long because the guy I was dating liked it better that way. But I *hated* it long. And look at it now," I laughed, tugging on the nonshiny hairs drooping over my eyes. "It's out of control!"

Joel stopped and turned to me, reaching his hand to my shoulder to examine me more closely. For a moment, I thought he might kiss me—or I him. I was a little confused by my sudden whirl of feelings. But instead of reaching down for a kiss, he looked at me kindly, and with approval. "I like your hair."

I felt myself squirm a little. I felt like he was looking into my soul and soothing my vulnerable, insecure self, which felt somehow even more intimate (but maybe not as awkward) as a sudden kiss. I could feel my cheeks blush as my finger tucked my hair behind my ear. I was startled into a bit of a swoon by his kind intensity and could barely speak. "Thank you."

Here I was, in the midst of trying to be my most authentic self, and I couldn't handle the attention that came with it. Joel's flattery, his proximity, suddenly made his status as a friend-with-potential much more real, but I surprised myself by feeling uncomfortable with the sudden intimacy, instead of elated. I wasn't ready for it. Or maybe the fantasy of him as a friend-with-potential was less threatening to my still-vulnerable heart. I focused once again on my footsteps, and picked up the pace.

"Well," he said, acting as if we hadn't just had a spark of uncertain romance, "you certainly seem much happier now than you did when I first saw you. I remember taking note of you. You seem more like . . . yourself now."

"I definitely *feel* more like myself these days," I admitted, feeling good about that truth.

"It took me a while before I got to know you," he said. And then he paused, as if debating how much to share. "I'm glad I got to know you, Tamara."

I felt nervous—even vulnerable and awkward. I wasn't sure I was comfortable with his sudden candor, and the possibility it suggested.

"I'm glad we became friends, too, Joel." I wasn't sure how he felt about my using the word "friends," but, in spite of my internal curiosity about him, I wasn't quite ready to go down that road. But he did help me push past my comfort level when it came to intimacy. Because even though his compliments made me nervous, I accepted his words with gratitude. And in turn, it made me more grateful for him. I stopped holding my breath and felt suddenly more liberated and in control of the moment—if not also my fate.

I stopped pretending to be the cool girl who could handle Arctic conditions. I let my teeth chatter freely as I pointed out the temperature sign to Joel. "Look!" I announced. "It is *six* degrees! It's *freezing* out here! And where, may I ask, are *your* gloves?"

"I forgot. But my coat is warm. See?" he said, shoving his hands in his pockets, "I can still keep my hands warm."

I dug into my purse and weeded out an extra pair of gloves I had tucked away in case I ever forgot mine. "Here. I know they're small, but at least try them on. Please! And here you were worried that *I* was cold! Joel, you're not even wearing a hat!"

We were back to being playful friends. For now, I was comfortable with that. As we backtracked across the bridge, we chatted amiably. Time would tell if we'd reached our full potential together.

DATE 3: CHRIS

Nothing could have prepared me for the moment I met one of my ex-boyfriend's doppelgängers. My friend Lumina (who is every bit as warm, artistic, and bright as her name sounds) warned me when she set us up. "He's hot, Tam. You'll like him. But there's something you should know . . . " she paused. "He kind of looks like . . . You Know Who."

Lumina was referring to my ex who always seemed more interested in his job and his car than he was in our relationship. The guy who preferred my hair long instead of short. He had me so twisted up inside, I could never figure out what he really wanted from me.

"I feel like you look at me as an *almost*," he said once. "Like those pictures where everything looks almost right, almost perfect, but it just isn't good enough." And that's how our relationship felt. Almost picture perfect.

I was willingly a mess and couldn't shake him, even after we finally broke up after a year. He was my last big love before Boring Guy, who didn't leave half the scar on my heart that You Know Who had. I figured I'd be okay when I met Date No. 3. But that still-shattered little place in my heart that prickled with chaos and angst came rushing back to haunt me when I finally met Chris, who was waiting for me outside Madison Square Garden, wearing a white Red Sox cap.

Lumina was right about Chris: He had my ex's dark Asian eyes, a deep-golden complexion, and strong shoulders that he carried with a confident stance. I felt a nervous dance in my belly as I approached him, unsure what to expect. Chris surprised me, opening his arms to me in a big friendly hug as if we were old friends reuniting after years apart. I felt my worries begin to dissipate.

"Welcome to New York!" I declared, beaming, and once again felt those first-date jitters.

Chris was visiting from Boston (which, coincidentally, was the hometown of You Know Who). *Please,* I begged myself, *don't spend the rest of the evening comparing their similarities.* Instead, I tried to focus on him as a new guy in my life, a mold all his own—not a shadow of my past love.

On a positive note, I finally managed to pay for the date after finding some cheap tickets to see the Knicks play basketball. Two tickets, $10 each. Well below my $31 limit—paid out of my own purse. What I didn't expect was how empowered it made me feel to spring for the date.

We followed the crowd past the concession stands, where the smell of overpriced buttered popcorn and hot dogs wafted our way. We funneled into the packed coliseum, which boomed with the announcer's voice, loud background music, and the high-pitched squeak of basketball shoes grinding against the court. We hiked to the highest seats in the stadium, which gave us a bird's-eye view of the action from the top rim of the crowd.

"Chris, I'm sorry these seats aren't so great."

"Are you *kidding?* Just *being* here is awesome. Madison Square Garden? Basketball? I mean, it *is* the Knicks, probably the worst team in the NBA," he teased. "But . . . nah, this is great!"

"Are you a big basketball fan?"

"Basketball? I love anything to do with sports. I'm more of a baseball guy, though. Die-hard Red Sox fan."

"And you dare announce that so loudly here in New York? Brave man."

"I know. It might be dangerous for me to be wearing this Sox hat in Yankees territory this weekend."

We made small talk, but it moved seamlessly from one topic to the next, and You Know Who was nowhere on the horizon. Chris put me at ease, a quality that's so easy to take for granted. So far, the old adage that three's a charm was living up to its promise.

"How long have you lived in Boston?" I asked, pleased that despite the exciting game below us, he was equally if not more engaged in our conversation.

"Boston? Just a few months this time around. I lived there for a long time as a kid, so it's kinda my home."

Chris and I talked during the entire game, mostly about dating. I found it easy to open up to him about my insecurities with this project, and my many frustrations and philosophies about dating. Before I knew it, I was unloading more information about myself than seemed appropriate for a first date. After all, conventional dating advice suggests it's best to avoid talking about ex-boyfriends when you meet a new guy. But he seemed open and interested, and there's nothing conventional about my project anyway.

"Sometimes I feel like I still date the same way I did back in high school."

"Oh yeah?" Chris said, raising an eyebrow. "How's that?"

"I don't really know what I'm doing. I fall too easily. I feel naive and wistful when I meet someone and hope he likes me. And in some ways, maybe it feels like high school because I still feel like the geeky sidekick to all the pretty girls. Sometimes I still feel like the weirdo and all the boys just want to date the biscuits."

Chris shook his head in confusion, and then laughed. "Biscuits?"

"Yeah. You know, those perfectly cute, peppy girls who are really adorable and fun and boys just flock to them? They're light, fluffy, they go with everything." I paused, "But . . . maybe not so much substance. You know. *Biscuits.*"

Chris laughed. "I've never heard that before! But I get it."

"It's true, though, isn't it? Sometimes I feel like . . . " *Are you still talking? Please stop unloading every single thought that's going through your head right now.* " . . . maybe I'm just not as cute as all those girls . . . " *What are you DOING? Are you really rattling off your every thought? Are you seriously letting him into your vault of insecurities? Have you forgotten you just MET him?!*

"Well," he said, not noticing my sudden battling thoughts, which must have been evidenced on my face, "If it makes you feel better, I totally consider myself a meat-and-potatoes kind of guy."

Just then the crowd erupted in cheers, and a few measures of music pounded through the stadium as people clapped along. The announcer yelled loudly, "Threeeeeeeeee, eeeeeeeeeeee!!!!!"

"Chris, what about you? Do you date a lot? Or is that too personal?"

"No, I'm an open book," he said. "I date, but I feel like I don't date in the traditional sense, like . . . go out on dates like this all the time. I mean, I've *had* girlfriends. Some have ended better than others." He kept his eyes on the game, unassumingly interrogating me about my past. "What about you?"

"I've had some nasty breakups in the last year or so."

And there it was. The moment that snapped me back to thinking about You Know Who and when we broke up—the first time.

That time, we were in the car when my ex suggested nonchalantly, "Maybe it would be better if we were just friends."

I turned my head, trying to read his inscrutable profile as he stared ahead at the road. Anger stampeded into my throat. "Are you really suggesting this as we're on the way to the airport to *meet my family?*"

In the beginning of our relationship, we had been so certain that we were "meant to be." We had similar interests—we were both in the news business, we loved movies, God, sushi, and singing, and we were even from the same hometown. We dubbed our introduction a cosmic turn, and determined the future was ours to conquer. But . . . we didn't share the same sense of humor. Our basic thoughts on how the world ran were different. It was evident that our shared interests weren't solid enough to build a strong relationship. I didn't think he felt I was a priority in his life, while he thought I focused too much on what was wrong with our relationship. We were at odds.

And there we were in the car, both angry, headed to the airport *and* a breakup.

I had no idea what to make of it. I had paid for his plane ticket. Any other wise, strong woman would have told him to shove it and would have marched to the plane by herself, chin up, pride on high. But I was no longer that kind of woman. I had become a shadow of myself. I felt defeated and unlovable and I wanted to prove that I could make our seemingly "destined" relationship work. I held on tightly, and in the process, my neediness smothered all that was once good.

Deep down I knew I should have run while I had the chance. I should have been grateful we weren't married. The longer we dated, the more depressed I became. The more unfamiliar I was with myself. I feared being alone. I felt stuck.

My girlfriends stopped listening to me complain. "Tam," they would gently remind me, "you don't marry someone based on his potential." They called him a narcissist.

Maybe. In my most angry moments I would come up with other insults. He was cruel, hurtful, and heartless. And then I would take a step back and force myself to hold myself accountable. I was giving too much. I treated our relationship with more respect than I dared give myself. Somehow I had decided we would remain together, despite our incompatibility.

And he wasn't even actually cruel. He just didn't want the same things I wanted. He just wasn't interested, no matter how much of my heart I put into it.

In many ways, accepting my own faults in the relationship was a much harder pill to swallow than calling him names. I pushed too hard. I refused to see the reality of our incompatibility. I changed my behavior to appear more like that of the woman I thought he wanted, instead of being true to myself. I held on to our potential so tightly that I smothered him. It was humbling.

After a year of dating him, I thought back to the strong, independent woman I once had been. Where had *she* gone? I had spent twelve months trying to convince a guy I was worth a damn. I finally realized I might not have convinced him, but it was time I convinced myself.

I chopped my hair off and rebounded with Boring Guy, and was now trying to understand what it's like to be a successful single woman.

I hoped I would get better at this.

I unloaded most of the details to Chris. I'm not sure if that was the best move on a first date, but I figured, *What do I have to lose? He lives four hours away. He knows I'm going out with a bunch of other men. Who knows if anything will happen with this guy anyway?*

Somehow, talking to him about my ex-boyfriends, my mess-ups, my insecurities, made me feel closer to him. And he was devastatingly attractive. And genuinely interested in what I had to say. If we kept up this easy flow of communication, I could easily see Chris as boyfriend material. But there I went again, falling too hard too quickly.

I'm not sure if I made the best move by oversharing with Chris, but either way, I was glad that I followed my intuition to be myself, rather than act out scripted behavior—even if some might consider it a technical foul.

The Knicks lost by ten points.

I, on the other hand, think I did a pretty good job staying on my game.

DATE 4: RYAN

I believe in miracles.

People keep asking me, "Do you *really* think you can get *thirty* guys to go out with you?" I force a confident "Of course!"

I actually have no idea how I'll find that many guys to fill my calendar. After all, it seems like only yesterday I felt lucky to land three dates in a *year*. And now I'm hoping for ten times as many in just one *month*? I have no choice: I have to have faith or I have to give up.

So far, I've been able to schedule the guys a couple days ahead with the help of my friends. But even with my best-laid plans, I expected to have some last-minute problems.

Ryan—whom I met through a friend of a friend—called me early Sunday morning to say he wasn't sure if he could make it for our date. We had plans to spend the morning checking out some of Harlem's famous gospel churches. He'd stayed late at work the night before, he said, and needed more sleep. He dozed off for a few more hours and we met later in the day, figuring we'd improvise and find something fun.

There's a heightened energy in Harlem. The weekend of our date marked the celebration of Martin Luther King Jr.'s birthday, and it was also just a few days away from the historic inauguration of Barack Obama as the first African American president. The neighborhood was popping with positive energy and excitement.

I met Ryan by my apartment in the heart of Harlem, right by 125th Street, and I was immediately struck by his kind smile and fluffy hair. He was just a tad taller than I was but stood strong, as if he were in charge of the whole neighborhood. Not conventionally handsome, but attractive by way of his demeanor.

Ryan was also a new transplant to New York, having moved three months prior from an all-white town in Michigan that had a population of thirteen thousand. He was ecstatic to be in an environment completely different from his own, and he wanted to see everything. For a guy completely out of his comfort zone, he adapted quickly. He smiled wide and cheerily said hello to strangers we passed as if he were a politician stomping for votes. He strutted along the sidewalk and announced loudly, "Harlem! I'm here!" The women walking by laughed and Ryan pulled his shoulders back in pride.

We stopped by the Studio Museum, which has free admission on Sundays, and admired the exhibits featuring local African American artists. We checked out the world-famous Apollo Theater, where Ryan suffered a case of hero worship when he saw "real-life New York City officers" standing outside. He asked them for hugs. They obliged, laughing at his enthusiasm and even posing for a picture with him. He also stopped to chat with the guys trying to sell him trinkets along the street.

He was nothing short of jubilant. And I quickly fell into a comfortable space with him, not overly pressured to chat, just enjoying exploring new streets through the eyes of an awe-struck small-town boy. It was charming. *I* was charmed.

We turned onto 116th Street and found ourselves among restaurants and bakeries, where the tempting aroma of fried chicken and warm bread drifted from the doorways. People crowded by the bus stops, bundled warmly, waiting to make their connection.

"Where do you think they're all going?" he asked with delight.

Ryan's enthusiasm was boundless, and he had the wide-eyed curiosity that seemed to come naturally to people from small towns. In our short time together, I could also tell that he had a positive attitude about life in general. Nonjudgmental, and not at all cynical. It was refreshing.

"So what'd you do for Christmas?" I asked, assuming his New York holiday had been quite different from the traditional Norman Rockwell Christmases I imagined he had celebrated in Michigan.

"I stayed here by myself."

His voice dropped a little, and for the first time that day, his demeanor was more somber. "I wanted to help at a home-less shelter or something, but by the time I had checked, all the volunteer spots were filled. So instead, I invited the homeless guy who lives near my apartment out for dinner."

Is this guy for real? I thought, my cynical city-girl radar going off. *Or is he just feeding me a line to seem compassionate?*

"So, there's this homeless guy I see every day. And on Christmas, I invited him to my place, offered him a shower, some new clothes, and took him out for dinner."

Whoa.

"You invited him into your *place?*"

"Yeah. It was fine. I *did* make a big mistake, though. I also gave him twenty dollars. Now he asks me for money *every day.* I used to give him a couple bucks when I saw him. But now he's started asking me for twenty dollars *every day.*"

"What do you say when he asks?"

"Well . . . now I just walk a different way to work every day."

Is he TOO nice? Maybe a pushover? This guy definitely hasn't learned the New Yorker's hardened habit of saying NO.

Just then Ryan reached down to the ground and picked up an empty plastic bag on the street—a typical element of New York's street scene. He held on to it until we passed a garbage can.

His conscientiousness was a stark contrast with the average New Yorker's busy self-involvement. In my rushed life, I felt like a considerate citizen because I recycled my *own* garbage, not somebody else's.

"Ryan, how did you come to look at the world the way you do?"

Ryan hesitated, and then he opened up about an accident that happened when he was eight years old. "You gotta understand," he said, "my mom still has a hard time even thinking about what happened. So I try not to make too big of a deal about it.

"But . . . " he paused, as if debating how much to reveal. "When I was a kid, I was riding in the family van. I was in the backseat without my seat belt on, and I was sitting in the middle—perched right between the driver's seat and the passenger's seat. It was raining and the roads were slippery. The van spun around and then squealed to a stop. That's when I flew headfirst out the windshield and landed in the middle of the street. When the ambulance arrived they pronounced me dead on the scene."

It's strange how, in a flash, everything you think you know about a person can be turned on its head—every assumption, every notion, every perspective you've balled together into this single impression of who a person is. Ryan wasn't a naive small-town boy with a Pollyana attitude. That's not what informed his profoundly gracious soul at all.

"I don't really remember a lot of the accident," he continued. "The next thing I knew, I was waking up in a hospital. Turns out I'd been in a coma for fourteen days.

"It took me a while to heal. I was sent to the best doctors in the state and spent four months in the hospital. I had to miss a lot of school. Instead I was tutored in the hospital. It was like I was in college at eight years old, going from class to class in a big building.

"I was lucky. I didn't have to relearn a lot. It just took a long time for me to recover physically. And I guess you gain a lot of perspective when you go through something like that."

I tried to imagine the anguish and hard work, the hope and sacrifice he and his family must have experienced. "I can see why your mom says that time in your lives is hard for her to think about."

What would that be like, I wondered, to wake every morning and see life as a miracle? We continued walking, both of us comfortably quiet as we shifted into our new intimacy. And then, as if guided by some spiritual compass, we turned a random corner and suddenly found what we'd been looking for—an *open* gospel church with an early evening service. Ryan and I turned to each other, wide-eyed, ecstatic. "No way," I said. "Let's check it out!"

He was only too happy to oblige.

We stepped into the brightly lit, warm interior and were welcomed by a crowd of smiling strangers who were talking and milling about, finding their way to their seats. The energy was upbeat and welcoming. We were obvious outsiders—the only white faces in the crowd and dressed casually in jeans, whereas everyone in the congregation was dressed their best. The women wore lacy dresses and the men looked sharp in their pressed suits.

Ryan walked into the church as if he belonged there.

An older man wearing a nametag that read DEACON DIXON approached us. "Welcome, friends! Will you be joining us tonight?" He reached out his hand to Ryan.

"We certainly will!"

Ryan explained how we had been hoping to find an open church in the neighborhood all day. "Deacon, do you happen to have gospel music at your evening service?"

The bishop's smile grew and his shoulders puffed with joy. "Oh, we have *lots* of music here. Best way to praise! Come find a seat!"

Ryan and I sat in one of the pews in the back, just as the service was beginning. The church was part chapel, part music hall. The sanctuary was large and bright. Ornate crosses and fresh people-size bouquets of flowers dressed the room, and a set of instruments shouldered each other near the pulpit.

The sound of an electric piano suddenly filled the room and the choir began singing. The entire congregation clapped along, praising, "Hallelujah!" One after another, people rose from their seats and shouted how much they loved the Lord and knew that God was good. They spoke of their challenges, their never-ending faith, and their gratitude for the community. "Praise Jesus!" one would shout. "Amen!" the rest would follow.

The joy of the people was like an electric energy pulsing through the room. I felt tears well up in my eyes as I soaked up the sweetness of my Harlem neighbors and the miracle of meeting someone inspiring like Ryan. I felt suddenly blessed in the realization that this project would teach me so much more about the process of dating. I felt a deep gratefulness that it could actually have a bigger impact on my life than I expected. I just needed to *allow* the lessons to happen, which I think is part of opening myself up to what another person has to offer—outside of the potentially romantic.

And then Ryan stood up.

He spoke boldly, and with gratitude. "I'm Ryan. I had to work until 6:00 AM and wasn't able to make it to church this morning. But we just found this service when we were walking by tonight. And I just wanted to say that I have never felt more welcomed in a church than I have in this one. So thank you."

Everyone clapped and cheered, "Welcome!"

The music seemed to grow louder. Ryan danced along with the crowd and sang his tone-deaf heart out. He clapped off beat. He shouted, "Amen!" and "Hallelujah!" with everyone around us.

I clapped softly and took in the power of the evening, thanking God and feeling the heavy pulse of my heart receiving the love around me.

Something seemed to be telling me that even more miracles were in store. . . .

DATE 5: ADAM

Amazing that I could go from such a transcendent, intimate experience in Harlem to what felt like the world record for the longest first date. And with how much sleep in between? Put it this way—it was less than half the length of my thirteen-hour foray with my fifth date, Adam. Even more amazing, I think I developed a pretty mad crush on him during our dozen-hour day.

Adam took me by surprise when I saw his name pop up on my phone. I'd met him briefly at a party when he moved to the city a year earlier. I thought he was cute and charming and we'd flirted—or at least *I* had—just long enough to exchange numbers, "in case anything fun came up." I was pretty sure he'd forgotten I even existed until a couple days ago. Apparently, he heard about my project through a friend, and his unabashedly excited voicemail made me blush a bit with excitement. I *had* made an impression, after all.

"Tamara!" he'd shouted, "It's Adam! Let's go out!"

I have to admit, it's validating to have someone sound so darn happy at the prospect of going out with me—especially someone I want to date. Since the project started, I've been getting varied reactions from guys. Some guys ignore my email requests completely. Others will write me back with a nice enough "no thank you," excusing themselves over concerns that it might make them look bad professionally. Other men admitted that they feared first dates to begin with, so the thought of being part of a project about first dates doubled their anxiety.

But for every guy who declined my open call, there were others eager to participate. Somehow, the idea of a girl offering a no-strings-attached first date—albeit a chaste one—was appealing. For them, it had the opposite effect: It took the pressure off. It was about having fun and being adventurous.

Is this why Adam's interested? I wondered, as I tried to temper my excitement. *Or is he interested in* me?

Adam had Monday off to mark Martin Luther King Jr.'s birthday, and I had scheduled the day off in the midst of my typically wonky workweek, which includes late shifts mixed with getting up in the middle of the night. Still, our day started *early*. We met up in Midtown, hoping to get tickets to see one of Conan O'Brien's final live tapings of his late-night show. Adam arrived at 7:00 AM, flashing his megawatt smile and toting bagels and cream cheese to share. But just as he arrived, the audience coordinators announced that no more tickets were available. *Bummer.*

I was crestfallen, but Adam was undeterred.

"Hey, there's tons of shows out there," he said. "Let's do our own tour of television shows!'"

I loved his can-do attitude. His fortitude. His atypical positive energy about everything at 7:00 AM. *Yep, I'm in trouble.*

As we wolfed down our fresh-baked bagels, we mapped out our impromptu stops and settled on a goal of trying to get tickets to see an afternoon recording of Comedy Central's *The Colbert Report.*

We hit up hot spots around the city, including CNN's New York headquarters near Columbus Circle, NBC's hub at Rockefeller Center, and ABC's home base at Lincoln Square—which was also where I worked. Feeling suddenly empowered, I took him inside and gave him a behind-the-scenes look at the *World News* set, where fellow producers and writers rushed to put the show together. I looked around nervously, wondering whether my coworkers could tell I was on a date. How would I introduce Adam? As my friend? My date? Some dude who agreed to go out with me since there were no strings attached?

"Can we take a picture on the set?" he asked.

"Of course!" I said, hustling into the studio to the news anchor's desk. I felt proud, as if I had a connection to something Adam thought was cool. Maybe he'd think I was cool, too.

I handed my camera to the floor director, who was checking the lights in preparation for the evening's show. "Sheryl, this is Adam"—just Adam. "Can you take a picture of us?" I moved close to Adam as he reached his arm around me, posing for the camera. I tucked my hand behind him, placing it on his back, noticing how comfortable I felt standing so close to him, tucked under his arm. *I could get used to this.*

I showed him my office, where I get to interview some of the world's most interesting people in preparation for the next day's show: authors about new books, real-life princesses, men who say they talk to Jesus, men who say they *are* Jesus, and people experiencing some of the most tragic, heart-wrenching events of their lives. And then there are the conversations with movie stars and other celebrities. Like the time Matthew McConaughey swooned me into having a crush on him in less than three minutes. Or the time *Desperate Housewives* hottie Marcia Cross took time to give me love advice ("Be hopeful!"). And boy, was I ever hopeful. I wondered, was I the only one feeling the comfortable flirtation with Adam, or was there actually something between us?

We left the studios behind and spent the afternoon traipsing through Greenwich Village, where we hit up several little treasures: Adam's favorite pizza spot; specialty shops for olive oil, cheeses, and cookies; and a beautiful, cozy Italian restaurant that, to our disappointment, was closed.

Adam gave me a sly look. "Do you want to see it?" he asked, a bit of a mischievous grin playing on his far-too-kissable lips.

"Well, yeah. But look, it's closed."

"I'll see about that." And with that, Adam rapped on the glass door, friendly but insistent. When the owner answered, Adam startled me with a sudden torrent of flawless Italian.

Whoa. Delizioso. Stick a fork in me. I'm done.

I think I may have actually swooned as I listened to Adam charm his way into a tour of the restaurant with his sultry Sicilian accent. The owners gave us a tour of the kitchen and invited us to take a look at the intimate patio. Seeing the ivy sweeping its way up the walls, the classic white wicker chairs, and the handsome men chatting in Italian, I felt like we'd been transported to some cobbled side street in Rome and Adam was my handsome Italian guide.

The effect was enhanced by Adam's smooth Italian as he exchanged pleasantries with the men. It was like chocolate to my ears, smooth and delicious. I was hypnotized by his mouth, the way his lips moved—how plump, pink, and sweet they looked. I imagined he was speaking about the azure coast of the Riviera and the country's fertile, grape-heavy vineyards. I felt entrenched in the romantic countryside of Italy—even wooed—but I was ripped from my daydream when Adam dropped suddenly back into English.

"Tamara. You ready to go? These guys say they're closed for the holiday."

I snapped back into the reality of New York City's busy side streets and frenetic pace. Definitely not languid Italy. Even though we had the entire day to explore, I felt hurried to get everywhere.

Adam constantly came up with random places to show me: a quaint shop with cheeses from around the world, where we tasted bits of fresh gouda and mozzarella. The building used in the opening credits of *Friends*. And his favorite place to get a slice in the city, Joe's Pizza.

"The crust is to die for," he said. "But if you hate it, you'll be honest, right?"

"Well, you haven't disappointed me yet," I said, nervous that he'd think I was sounding too flirtatious.

"I hope I don't ever," he said, flirting back.

It's no surprise that my crush on Adam grew as the day progressed. It's not just because he's good-looking, it's also his positive, boisterous, adventurous personality: Being around him makes me happy. His smile shows off his perfectly aligned, sparkling teeth, matching his bright personality. He was practically born snowboarding. He's traveled the world. He has his pilot's license. He's been skydiving and bungee jumping. And he's twenty-five.

"Twenty-five?" I asked, a little startled. I hadn't realized he was that much younger—he had the air of someone older. "So . . . " I said, feeling a little empowered as the cool, older woman, "I'm thirty-one. Should I feel old?"

"I don't think so," he said, with a playful look. "We're just a few years apart. I don't think you're old enough to qualify as a cougar or anything." He gave me a challenging look, flirty but friendly.

"Oh!" I said blushing. "So, how old does someone need to be for her to be considered a cougar?"

He took a second, contemplating his answer. "Forties? Fifties?"

Hmmm. Would that make me a kitten, then? That was certainly more alluring. I continued our repartee.

"And what if you're *older?* Like, a really, really old chick on the prowl. What are you then?"

"A saber-tooth."

We both laughed, enjoying the easy banter. "Nice one!" I said, giving him an approving nod. *Oh, how I love witty men.*

We traipsed through the city all day. It was exhausting but fun, and I quickly shed my go-to front of being the "cool girl on a first date." With Adam, I didn't feel the need to put on an act. I felt relaxed and completely myself around him. It just felt natural to be that way. And isn't that at the heart of intimacy? If things were ever going to work out romantically with anyone in my life, I wanted the relationship to feel legitimate and real.

For his part, Adam seemed equally at ease. We laughed together and seemed to easily play off each other's comments. But I couldn't tell if he felt some sort of romantic attraction to me or if I were more like his funny sidekick. He would laugh and smile, sometimes flirting with me, but he didn't seem to give me those big signals to indicate whether he liked me. No looking deeply into my eyes. No obligatory moments of touching my arm. No overtly flattering comments. I couldn't pinpoint if I was the only one with a crush.

As we made our way into the studios of *The Colbert Report,* the snow started to fall. Our constant need to talk seemed to quiet. I wondered what he was thinking about as he paced side to side, looking into the street. Had he tired of me? Was he waiting for the date to be over? Or was he just cold and hoping to get inside? I could feel my insecurities creeping back, and I tried to act like a cool girl again. I tried to watch him without watching him, looking at him from the corner of my eye.

"It's so cold!" he said, still smiling.

Once inside the studio, we sat down, happy to get off our feet. We melted into our seats and sighed with pleasure, laughing at our mutual contentment. We chitchatted comfortably and watched producers and the crew scurrying around the set, prepping for the show. I did my best to explain what they were doing—rushing scripts onto the set, yelling cues out to one another on their headsets—the general frenzied game-face fury I'd become all too familiar with over my years of working in television.

As we watched the hustle-bustle, I felt my body relax into the chair—feeling comfortable beside Adam. I thought of the long day we'd spent exploring the city and how this dating project was much like this show prep.

When it comes to television, a lot goes on behind the scenes. That's where all the hard work begins. By the time it's showtime, either you've been prepared enough to have fun with your work or it's a struggle to get through. That's what this dating project feels like. The more prepared I feel—and by that I mean comfortable in my skin, relaxed in my intentions, focused on my best interests and the true character of the person beside me, not the knee-jerk hope for a potential relationship—the more I get to have fun on the dates.

In the past, I felt like I was working *during* the dates—to be alluring, to impress, to seduce him through charm. I'd put on my coolest attitude. Act as if nothing in the world bothered me. Get overly excited about everything we talked about. Flip my hair. Touch his elbow. Laugh at his jokes—even the dumb ones.

Now, I'm starting to realize the importance of simply being *present*. The less time I spend worrying about how dumb/cool/pretty I'm looking, the more genuine I feel and the more fun I have.

And I felt that authenticity with Adam. As for him? Was he on this date for the adventure or for me? Maybe a little of both. And that was okay, because I suddenly realized that what mattered weren't his intentions, but my own.

DATE 6:
EVAN

To: YOU!!!
Subject: SOS!!!

Hey friends!

Guess what? Apparently I got my times
confused for my date tonight and . . .
whoops! My theater tickets aren't booked
for an 8:00 PM show but for 7:00!!! Now
my date can't make it! I'm freaking
out, as I only have a few hours to find
someone to fill the spot. Can you help
find me someone to bail me out? If not,
I'm fully prepared to walk across the
street to Starbucks and hand out my
business cards, but I'd prefer to go out

with someone you know. Any thoughts on someone available for tonight?

Thanks in advance for saving me!!!

I sat staring at my computer, paralyzed with panic. My heart raced and my eyes bulged as I stared at my inbox and waited for a response. *How could I have overlooked such an important detail as the start time of this play? Who starts a play at seven o'clock?!*

It was 3:30 PM, and I had only a few hours to find a replacement guy. *Replacement guy?* How funny. I'd spent how many years looking for Mr. Right? And now I expected some new guy—Mr. Right or not—to show up in mere *hours,* simply because I *asked?* Hmmm. Even though I was in a total panic about not meeting my daily quota, I kind of liked my new outlook. My expectations now were about the date—not whether it would take me down the aisle. I wasn't fantasizing about a perfect life for me and Adam in Italy (why not!), waiting by the phone, distracted into neurosis wondering if he was my last-chance hero of wedlock. This, I thought, was progress.

But still. I should have planned ahead. My friends had been asking me, "What if someone ends up not being able to make it?" and I would jokingly respond, "I'll just have to ask someone off the street," but I never thought I would have to actually put that plan into effect.

How could I have let this happen? And so early in the project!

I was feeling enough stress as it was, because in addition to juggling my regular forty-hour-a-week gig, I now had three extra *self-inflicted* part-time jobs:

1. WRITER: Every night, after coming home from these dates, I'd spend a couple hours writing notes about how our date went, and then post them online.

2. DATER: It's funny to think of dating like a job, because the most important element I've learned so far is to set aside all my cares and just have fun on the date. Still, going out every day requires the bulk of my time and energy.

3. PRODUCER: Finding guys to go out with, coming up with fun date ideas, and scheduling these dates requires the same tenacity and ingenuity that a producer employs in filling out a news or talk show. Until now, I'd been managing this part of it pretty well.

I weighed my options. I could give up and quit my entire project. I could go to the theater by myself and hit on a single-looking guy there. I could approach someone on the street, or I could see if one of my coworkers would go with me.

Here was my plan: First, allow myself thirty minutes to freak out about my crisis. Then, if no one pulled through, grab my business cards, hit Starbucks, and panhandle for a man.

I felt a wash of panic at the thought. *Oh, crap.*

As I attempted meditation breaths, I thought about my predicament. This whole project was about choice, I realized. And here I could choose to look at this blip in my scheduling as a scary challenge or an opportunity. Maybe, just maybe, this challenge was put in my way to test me, I thought further. It certainly forced me to consider how important it was that I commit to finishing the project.

I took in a few more deep, meditative breaths and tried to think of clouds. Or, wait—was I supposed to think of a gently rolling ocean? As I worked out the equivalent of a calming screen-saver for my mind, I noticed a new email pop up in my inbox from a buddy of mine, Matthew.

> Tamara—I sent an email to my friend Evan and told him about you and a little about your project. He'd love to go. Evan's the bomb. If you haven't met him, he's the coolest surfer boy you'll ever meet. Evan = cool date.

Right away, I knew I'd like Evan. First, any guy willing to sign up for my social experiment gets my immediate respect. In Evan's case, I was especially grateful that he not only was bailing me out at the last minute, but also seemed intrigued and excited.

I was sitting in the lobby when I saw him walk in, looking around for me. He looked a lot like the guys I would have fallen for instantly in college: tall, blue eyes, strong shoulders, and an inviting smile that I noticed when I caught his eye.

"Evan?" I asked, standing to meet the man who'd come to my rescue for the evening. "Thank you so much. You realize you've instantly become my hero," I said, flirty and grateful.

"No problem," he said. "I just had to cancel all the other dates I had lined up for the evening," he joked as we walked into the theater. "Totally worth the sacrifice."

As the lights began to dim, I whispered to him, "Sorry in advance if this show sucks. I hope you don't mind—it's a musical."

Evan's eyes beamed with delight. "That's okay. I *love* musicals!"

Loves musicals? I looked at him curiously as the music began. *Is this guy gay?*

The show, *Sessions,* was about a bunch of people in group therapy. After my stressful day, I was definitely a candidate for some therapy, even if it was vicarious—and fictional. Unfortunately, the performance turned out to be pretty awful. With a single piano to accompany the actors, *and* the flat singing, it came off little better than a junior high school musical (no offense to hard-working twelve-year-olds doing *The Wizard of Oz).* I tried my best to tolerate the singing, but it was painful to listen to—even watch. I felt both annoyed and sympathetic. Evan clearly felt the same. At particularly cringe-worthy moments in the play, we'd share expressions of commiseration: pained looks, eye rolling, and grimaces of empathy. *Oh, those poor actors! Oh, poor us!*

It got so bad, we began passing notes back and forth, critiquing choice moments. We were like two kids snickering in the back of class. I felt so comfortable around him. Totally at ease. Totally myself. When the show ended—none too soon—we headed outside. I feared we'd have one of those awkward moments when meeting someone without plans, trying to figure out if we would spend more time together or part ways. But Evan casually offered to extend our evening.

"So, do you have plans now? Or would you mind heading uptown with me? Maybe we could get some dessert?"

"I'm totally game for whatever," I said, excited to spend more time with him while forgetting about my 3:00 AM wake-up call for work. My sleep would once again be necessarily sacrificed.

We headed to Morningside Heights, by our shared stomping grounds, Columbia University, where Evan was finishing his master's degree in "quantitative methods in the social sciences."

"Sounds really snooty," I said, teasing.

"I'm pretty sure just saying the name of the program makes me smarter," he mused.

We stopped by a bakery for a couple cookies and some hot chocolate to warm us up. "I love black and white cookies," he said, biting into one. "Tastes so good!" he said, as if cheering the cookie for its existence.

I laughed, feeling a level of comfort with him that I hadn't felt in a long time. I instantly liked and respected him. As we walked across the grand, quiet campus, Evan told me about his world travels, how he'd spent time surfing in Peru and Panama, and how he'd managed to live in Hawaii, Tonga, and Ecuador.

Evan seemed smart and engaging. It was hard to imagine his living a vagabond surfer existence. Because here he was, pursuing his master's degree at Columbia while working part-time for a market research company back in California—where (of course) he grew up surfing with his brothers. I have to admit, when I think of surfers, Evan's not exactly the kind of person who comes to mind. Admittedly, I buy into the stereotype that surfers are a little bit delusional and out of touch with reality—like those guys in *Bill and Ted's Excellent Adventure*.

Evan certainly proved me wrong. Another good lesson, filed for future reference: *Do not make assumptions based on ignorance.*

Check.

"Do *you* travel?" he asked, curious but not challenging.

"I haven't been on a real trip in forever. But I'd love to go back to Ireland," I gushed. "That place must be greener than anywhere else on Earth, I swear. And the grass is so soft it's like walking on pillows!"

We both laughed at that image, and Evan smiled. Our eyes met and lingered. I felt a spark in the space between us.

"Sounds like a place I'd like to visit," he finally said.

Good thing we were walking, or I swear I might have leaned in for a kiss.

"Have you ever been to the top of any of the buildings?" he asked.

"Are we allowed to?" I asked, feeling like a teenager, nervous we'd get in trouble.

"I never asked," he said with a smile. "You up for it?"

I nodded with a wide grin, feeling as if Evan was the perfect partner for any adventure. He led me through the campus, past the architecture buildings and up to a secret spot on top of one of the business buildings. We crept up to the roof, where ice was left over from a recent snowfall. Evan pointed to a high step, reached for my hand, and helped me up onto a ridge so I could see the entire cityscape twinkling below us. The view was clear all the way north to the George Washington Bridge and down to Midtown, where the Empire State Building stood tall, watching protectively over the rest of the city.

"It's like you can see the whole world from here," I said. I was genuinely awestruck—by the view, by him.

"Yeah, I love this spot," he said, as he settled himself beside me. He was quiet, but a small smile of what seemed like contentment played at the corner of his lips.

As I soaked in the view and the ease of the moment, I found myself feeling as if Evan and I were old friends, picking up where we had left off years before. On the surface, we seemed so different: He loves to be in the water, while I barely avoided drowning in the kiddie pool. He loves to cook, and I'm pretty sure my stove would catch fire from all the dust it's collected. But we seemed to share similar viewpoints on faith, politics, family, and even dating. Suddenly all those lists I had made popped into my head, and I realized how well he aligned with my imaginary ideal man: tall, curly dark brown hair, blue eyes. He made me laugh. He even spoke Spanish and played the guitar. And he was kind enough to pay for my cab ride home. Somehow, in my constant seeking, I had come to believe men like Evan didn't exist.

I could seriously see myself falling in love with this guy.

Was I really allowing myself to think these thoughts on a first date? Was I falling into my old habits again or was something special really there?

We headed back down to ground level (I definitely felt like I needed to get my head out of the clouds) so I could go home and get to bed. A cab came down the street and Evan put his two fingers to his mouth and ripped a loud whistle, to which the cab promptly stopped. "I had a really great time tonight," he said, reaching in to hug me with his strong embrace.

"I'm so glad things worked out the way they did," I said.

I stepped into the cab and Evan handed me a $20 bill. "I hope this covers your ride home," he said, flashing me a smile before shutting the door behind me.

I went home and managed to squeeze in a few hours of sleep before heading to work at 3:00 AM. When I logged on to the computer, I saw an email waiting for me—from Evan.

Subject: FW: Last-minute deal to Ireland

Tamara,
Thanks for the great night. I saw this travel deal and thought of you. Hope you got some sleep before heading into work.

-Evan

What if he likes me?!
Good question, self, because I think I could really like *him*.

Ciao, Italy. Looks like the luck of the Irish might be taking the lead.

DATE 7: JARED

SEVEN (NOT SO) DEADLY SINS OF DATING:
1. Humiliation

"Don't be surprised if I fall right away," he said, stepping cautiously onto the ice.

"I thought all guys from Minnesota knew how to ice skate," I teased.

"That's ice *hockey*," he corrected with a "gotcha" grin. "Totally different skates than figure skating. These skates," he added, pointing to the jagged blade on his boot, "these have *toe picks*. It takes a little getting used to."

"I'm sure you'll be fine," I said, hoping not to be the first one to fall.

"You wanna bet?"

Jared reached out for my hand, a bit hesitantly, and helped me onto the ice. A bunch of seven-year-olds swished by, giggling and chasing each other around the rink. We took a few small, awkward steps and tried to glide. All of a sudden Jared's legs flew out from under him and he flailed his arms wildly, trying to catch himself before landing on his back. I let out a light gasp and reached for him. "Are you okay?!"

"Yeah," he said, slowly pushing himself back up to standing. He was blushing fiercely, but laughing too. "I think I hurt my pride the most."

I dusted the clumps of shaved ice off the back of his coat. "Well, I really appreciate you falling first. That was really gracious of you."

"Anything I can do to help," he said, wiping his hands. He gestured toward a little girl in a pink puffy jacket with brown pigtails swishing past him. "Maybe I should take a few lessons from her."

We both laughed, and though he was handling it all with grace, I hoped he wasn't too embarrassed. "You ready to try again?"

"*Oh* yeah," he said, and he grabbed my hand.

2. Lethargy

Jared was still amazed that I'd made it to our early afternoon date after the full day of work I'd already managed to fit in. After my playdate with Evan, I'd gone home to write a bit, crashed for a couple hours, gotten up, gone to work at 3:00 AM, and then headed to pottery class just before meeting up with Jared for our 11:00 AM date.

Yes, pottery. I thought the class would be fun and creative and would help me feel a little more Zen by bringing balance to my go-go-go attitude. Instead, I just rush through class and make crappy mugs.

"Hey . . . where's my clay pot?" Jared chided when we first met. He'd arrived bundled in warm clothes and presented me with a megasize can of a superpowerful energy drink, tied in a yellow bow. "I figured you'd be tired, so I wanted to make sure you stayed awake for our date."

I liked his charm.

We started picking up the pace on the ice, finally getting into our groove enough to feel like we were keeping up with the tweens twirling in front of us. "So Jared, you moved here, what . . . three weeks ago?"

"Just last week, actually."

"Last week?! And you're already on a date? You move fast!"

"Yeah. I've been pretty lucky so far."

Jared had learned about my project from my friend Kat, who'd met him at an audition for a play.

"So, how's the auditioning going?"

"I have another one tomorrow. Pretty nervous, actually. It's for a pretty big theater."

"Just bring presents like you did with me and you'll be a shoo-in."

Despite my fatigue, I found it easy to banter with him. Still, I really couldn't wait till that energy drink kicked in. *Any minute now . . .*

3. Vanity

Jared is way cuter than Kat described: tall with broad shoulders, a light freckled complexion, piercing green eyes, and strawberry blond locks that drift lightly onto his brow.

I, on the other hand, looked like a hobo. I had been nervous the skating rink would be really cold, so I packed on a few layers of clothes: a pair of leggings under my jeans, and a shirt and a sweater under my heavy jacket. I was hoping to pull off that cute "snow bunny" look, but I looked more like a snowman. Not to mention my generally haggard-looking complexion from lack of sleep. Hopefully, Jared would be just as forgiving as he was handsome.

Somehow—despite all my layers—I managed to keep my cool skating next to him.

"Have you lived in Minnesota your whole life?"

"Nah, I spent some time in Alaska, too. And South Dakota."

"Oh yeah? I've never been to either," I said, trying to look effortless in my attempt to stay upright. "I imagine all that land must be really beautiful. Those states have *so much* space."

"Yeah," he said. "So far New York is *way* different."

"*Totally* different. The city's so crowded. But it has its own beauty. I bet you'll grow to love it."

Or *me*, for that matter, given the chance—but without a winter's worth of dowdy layers.

4. Piety

Jared grew up Lutheran and his dad was a Catholic. "Our family wasn't totally religious, but we were faithful and happy," he admitted, as we skated slowly around the rink, getting our "ice legs."

"Our family was a little like that, too," I said. I felt a little nervous as I rattled off my smorgasbord of religious affiliations. "My mom's a Protestant, my dad was agnostic, and my step-dad was a Catholic. I was raised Methodist, went to a Lutheran college, sang in the Presbyterian choir, and considered myself a pagan. And sometime in my twenties I became a Mormon."

He smiled in amusement. "You've had quite an exploration of religions," he teased. "I'm pretty open-minded about that kind of stuff. I pretty much think there's truth in everything."

"Me too."

We spent nearly an hour skating around the ice and talking openly about our current philosophies and the paths we've chosen in life. We met eye to eye, both believing in God, truth, happiness, and life's fullest possibilities. No matter what religion or dogma we each claimed, it seemed as if we easily accepted each other for who we were at our core, respecting each other for our good intentions.

5. Marriage

I leaned down and unlaced my skates. I wiggled my toes, trying to adjust my feet to the little bit of freedom that followed. I had stowed my shoes away in a nylon bag I'd rented. When I took my shoes out, I noticed something small and silvery fly out and fall next to my foot. I stared, wide-eyed, at the shiny object, digesting the reality of what lay before me. I reached down and delicately picked up what was just as I had suspected: a very expensive wedding band. The ring was beautiful, with perfect diamonds laced all around its edges. I looked at it carefully, examining the design and wondering about the purpose of its arrival in my life at that very moment. Why had a wedding band fallen at my feet? And why now—in the midst of my search for understanding more about . . . everything?

I rolled the band between my fingers, pondering its presence. *Did this just pop up out of nowhere? Is this a sign? Am I going to marry Jared? Or someone else from this crazy project?*

"Jared," I said, holding my gaze on the small fractals of light shining off the tiny diamonds. "I think I just found, um, a *wedding* ring."

Part of me wondered if this was some trick the universe was playing on me, mocking me for my attempt to understand love, men, and the complexities of relationships. It wasn't long ago that I'd been seriously debating my own desire for marriage.

I'd uttered what felt defiant at the time: "I don't want to get married." It felt good to get the words out and feel how they resonated with me. I feared being trapped in a marriage that was boring, or abusive, or destined for failure. I'd accepted the idea of being single. It felt empowering to realize I had the choice to marry or not, despite cultural expectations. It was liberating to stop holding up my marital status as a measure of the spectrum of my joy and happiness. But if the opportunity to spend the rest of my life with someone smart, funny, and kind presented itself, I would be forever grateful.

Still, when I held that ring and recognized what it truly signified—not submission, or deference, or old-school patriarchy, but the promise of being connected for life to someone against the backdrop of mutual, egalitarian love—I felt a strange loneliness.

Will I ever wear a ring like this?

6. Destiny

I stood up and tried to regain my balance, commanding my brain to send signals to my feet so they'd remember how to walk without skates. They felt strangely light as I walked to the rental counter.

"Ummm. Excuse me? Do you have a lost and found?" I held the ring delicately and pushed it close to the cashier's face, as if its proximity would help her understand the intense impact the ring had on me.

"Did you just *find* this?" she asked.

I guess.

Or maybe it found me. Isn't that what everyone says about the way things work with marriage—that somehow it's fate? Don't love and marriage just "find their way" to you? Isn't that belief the source of all the annoying uninvited advice my married friends have been telling me for years? *It happens when you least expect it.*

So, what was this? Fate or coincidence? Maybe it was simply up to me to decide . . .

7. Coveting

Jared and I walked to Grand Central Station and grabbed my favorite wintertime drink, hot chocolate. Its warm, rich flavor on a cold day makes me happy, contented. And as we soon discovered, it also goes really well with a piece of cheesecake.

"So," he said, probing about my dates, "are you prepared for guys asking you the same questions over and over again?"

"Not really," I said, diving into my slice. "You can probably relate to this. Back when I used to act, I always knew that no matter how many times I performed a show, it was always the first experience for the audience. So even though I might be asked similar questions along the way, it'll still be the first time being asked by a new person. Like, I've been ice skating before, right? But never with you, Jared," I flirted.

For the last few hours of our date, Jared and I chatted about human nature, theater, and what drives people to do what they do. I was fascinated by him.

As I listened to him open up about his hopes for his life in New York City, I realized the unexpected side effects from this dating project: I was starting to really like some of these guys. Adam, Evan, and now Jared . . . they each had a spark that made me a little more inspired about life—and about the potential for love.

I was beginning to feel hope about my future with men. I could envision becoming friends with them, perhaps even date a few again. Or not. I was simply happy in the moment.

And better, I was starting to *like* them—without expectation. The project was working.

DATE 8:
ALLEN

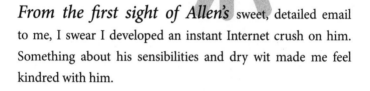

From the first sight of Allen's sweet, detailed email to me, I swear I developed an instant Internet crush on him. Something about his sensibilities and dry wit made me feel kindred with him.

Tamara,

I am so sorry for not getting back to you sooner. Tonight is the first night since our first email exchange that I was able to read up on your project and get a better idea of what I'm in for. I have to admit that when I told my friend Kelly that I was up for anything, I had no idea the extent of how much time you are devoting to this month. How can you do it? I applaud your effort and find this venture incredibly fascinating.

Now that I am a little more settled

in and not sleeping on my college room-mate's hardwood floors (my roommate failed to mention that the air mattress given to me was bereft of any structural integrity and was the same mattress used during his Boy Scout years. In addition, he failed to mention that the last time he USED it was ALSO in Boy Scouts!), I wanted to take some time to say hello.

To give you a little background in-formation, I was born in Dallas, raised in Oklahoma, and have now made my way to New York, with a brief stint in Scottsdale, Arizona. My little brother is my best friend in the whole world and not a day goes by that we do not at least text one another.

I recognize that there is injustice in the world and attempt to make a con-certed effort to battle this as often as I have time. I love well-prepared meals and nice dinners, but at the same time, I think peanut butter is my favorite substance on the planet, minus peanut butter with salmonella. I am not a crazy reformer, nor left- or right-wing activist, but at the same time I am not apathetic to the painful world we live in. I am an environmentalist, but I would never tie

myself to a tree during deforestation.
Are you CRAZY?!
I am terrified of heights.

Would meeting Allen in person change my feelings? Enhance them? I was both excited and nervous, and I was also a little conflicted by the affinity I already felt toward a few of my other first dates—Adam, Evan, Jared. How could so many great men suddenly just be present in my life? It was amazing and irritating at the same time. Talk about a test of will. I had to temper the urge to throw caution to the wind, declare a freeze on the dating project, and see where one of those first dates took me. But this was the whole point of the project, right? To gain enough insight and perspective about not only dating but also myself before diving into an insta-relationship? I have to admit, it was driving me a little crazy. And by the end of the date, given all I ended up revealing to Allen, I had to wonder if some of my impulses to hang on to men had something to do with my upbringing—which was a little crazy, and a little sad.

We met near Lincoln Center, just after I finished my workday. He'd mentioned he'd be wearing a long, tan wool coat, which seemed to be what every man in his late twenties was wearing that evening. But I could tell who Allen was by his dark blond shaggy locks and his blue eyes constantly scanning the postwork crowd, his head bobbing as if he were looking for someone. I'd finally met enough new guys that I seemed to lose that fear of approaching someone new. I walked behind him and tapped him on the shoulder. "Allen?"

"Hey!" he said, smiling, a little startled, and gave me a hug.

As we talked, I discovered that he's a patchwork of surprising qualities. He studied philosophy in college and graduate school, thinking he would go into teaching, but went into marketing artwork instead; he even taught guitar for a while. I discovered, too, that he's a bit impulsive, but he's also an old-school gentleman with traditional tastes. And he surprised me with his candor. It was refreshing.

"I didn't really like the students," he said, biting into his grilled cheese sandwich. He had gone out of his way to track down a good sandwich bar by my office, which had landed us at a small café in the Time Warner building.

"You didn't like the *students?*" I asked. "Isn't that essential for teaching?"

"Yeah, that's why I quit. I used to teach high school kids how to play guitar. It was so great when I saw that bright look in their eyes when they finally *got it*. But college students are different. They didn't seem as excited about learning as I hoped they would."

My forehead tightened in curiosity as I watched him. *He's smart, hardworking, cares about the world*, I thought. *And he's a nice guy. I think he might be a little like that grilled cheese sandwich: classic and simple.*

Given the choice, most people would probably pass up the grilled cheese sandwich on a menu full of other sandwiches in favor of something less ordinary and basic, say, a French dip or a hot pastrami.

On first blush, women might also consider Allen's low-key presence and midwestern looks "too ordinary," but he's anything but. Truth be told, he's likely the better option than all the flashier guys who claim to be "French dips."

"So you gave up teaching to go into marketing?" I asked.

"Yeah. It's different. Mostly I do it because I love the people I work with."

Allen is a solid guy from good stock. He grew up in Oklahoma, where his father is a Methodist pastor and his mother a caring adventurist. He blames her for his good manners.

Case in point: He scoffed when I offered to pay for dinner. He insisted on pulling out my chair, helped me with my coat, and even walked on the street side of the curb.

As we walked down Seventh Avenue toward Times Square to watch a comedy show, Allen offered me his arm. Despite being so attentive, he admitted to being generally distracted. "I have a pretty bad case of attention deficit disorder, so I'm used to people laughing at my expense."

I wasn't sure if he was joking or serious, and I was afraid to ask, for fear of offending him. Frankly, it didn't matter: Any guy who can earn a PhD in philosophy *and* hold chivalry in high regard can be as ADD as he pleases, as far as I'm concerned.

He wasn't afraid to open up to me about the rest of his personal life, sharing his relationship mishaps—like the time he proposed to a woman after only six weeks of dating.

"I'm historically a mess when it comes to women," he admitted.

"Allen," I probed, "are you one of those guys who goes out with someone for a while, gets dumped, and then a few months later your ex realizes what a horrible mistake she made and wants to get back together with you?"

He looked at me, eyes wide with astonishment, as if I had read his soul. *"All* the time."

"They think you're too nice?"

He thought for a second. "You could say I get into trouble when girls find out I'm really a Southern gentleman—minus the accent."

"Girls are crazy," I conclude.

"Yeah, I guess. But guys can be, too. Actually, my *family* is pretty crazy."

"Mine too!" I say with pride.

"We try to act like we're normal," he adds. "Don't get me wrong, I l*ove* them, but we have some baggage."

And then I found myself breaking my own personal rule of dating that I've had ever since I was twenty: Don't talk about your family baggage on the first date. But I felt as if I were in a safe zone with Allen as I whizzed through the bullet points of crises in my family:

- My parents divorced when I was five
- Because my dad was an alcoholic
- Dad struggled to quit drinking
- Mom remarried when I was twelve
- Two years later, my stepdad was diagnosed with cancer

- He died when I was sixteen
- A few months later, my dad was diagnosed with cancer
- He died when I was eighteen
- That was my lowest point

I felt an instant moment of regret. *Did I just unload too much personal information?* I looked to see whether Allen looked overwhelmed and hoped he wouldn't respond with that common, cynical roll of the eye that some people tend to have when women talk about their painful pasts involving their fathers. Allen's face remained calm and warm.

"Wow," he said. "As if being a teenager weren't hard enough. You watched *two* parents die of cancer?"

I felt accepted. As if my baggage wouldn't stand in the way of our new friendship . . . or whatever else might follow. Allen asked about my dad, and he seemed genuinely interested, so I shared . . .

My father was a phenomenal friend and a hardworking, brilliant, award-winning photojournalist. He also happened to be an alcoholic. Sometimes he would drink too much to realize I was sitting next to him. He would lose focus, forget everything, get scary angry, pass out, wake up, and forget everything again. Sometimes months would go by without our talking.

Then there were the times when he was sober: He was genuinely kind, hilarious, and as friendly as one could be. I gave him the benefit of the doubt, realizing that he was just another human being going through a struggle.

Growing up with an alcoholic taught me how to reflect on my needs and actions. I learned to quickly assess behaviors and personalities around me, feeling out if I was in a "safe" environment. Twelve-step jargon became the native tongue of our family.

What seemed to have the greater effect on my life—and my relationships with men—was the death of my stepdad, Keith, and then my dad.

Keith was diagnosed with cancer just as I began really warming up to him, just when I could admit that I loved him as a parent. I felt betrayed by God.

Our home turned into a hospital ward. Nurses would come by to help us take care of him. Talk of chemotherapy and radiation replaced discussions about schoolwork. He died right before my senior year of high school.

I was angry at everyone. I stopped talking to many people, including my father, for several months. I wanted him to reach out to me, to tell me he loved me, to fill that void—to be a *father*. I thought he had forgotten about me. And then I discovered that he'd been silent all those months because he was beginning treatment for his own cancer. My soul twisted inside me and settled like a knot in my stomach. *Why!* I screamed to the universe. He had quit drinking and smoking a few years before, but his many years of being victimized by his vices had done their damage.

Somehow, my dad's diagnosis helped improve our relationship. We made each other a priority. He lived alone and I lived nearby. It made sense that I would visit him frequently and take care of him the best I could. I would learn, once again, the gift of taking care of a dying parent.

Just as with Keith, I was able to see the humble, caring soul that dwelled in my father. Our moments together became precious gifts. Time after time, I would feel déjà vu as he lingered near death. With Keith, I had arrived at the hospital in my prom dress, knowing he would miss seeing me head off to one of the big events in my life. With my dad, I arrived at hospice in my high school cap and gown before my graduation.

Once again, I sat up late at night and listened to the beeping of the heart monitor machine. I would sleep lightly, listening closely to each breath, wondering if the long spans of silence were signaling death. I would stroke his thinning hair to the side of his face. He would tell me he cared about me. And I would smile with warming tears filling my eyes. Eventually, I would find myself at yet another funeral, again at Arlington National Cemetery, with that familiar twenty-one-gun salute hailing entry into hallowed grounds.

There was a long time in my life when those series of events seemed to define me. I felt as if I were God's personal joke. I was the only person I knew who had spent most of her teenage years taking care of dying parents. Somehow, I wondered if the deaths of my father and stepfather were just a horrible foundation for my relationships with all men: Were they all destined to leave me just as I started to feel closest to them? Was I drawn to creating immediate relationships with promising men for fear of losing them? It took me years to accept that disappointments and unfortunate events from my childhood and teenage years didn't have to dominate me or define who I was forever. My project had a deeper purpose as well, I realized as I shared with Allen: I was taking control of myself. I was defining *me,* in the present.

Part of my pattern when I became intimate with men was to share the trials of my family. But more often than not, it turned out to be a mistake. I would open up to guys too quickly and tell them all my secrets, my flaws, and my pains. And then I'd wonder, *Will you like me in spite of all this?* I would then develop a false sense of emotional intimacy, when really, if we were meant to be together, he would accept me as I was. I spent too much time putting men on a pedestal simply for not bolting the moment I revealed my true self, when I should have been more attuned to how our relationship flourished— or not—despite my past, or even because of it. Still, whenever a man ended our relationship, I would always wonder if it was because I had shared my past so early in the courtship.

And that's exactly how I was starting to feel with Allen. *Why* was I telling him all this stuff about my family? I would have to work hard to focus more on Allen and get to know him better. I didn't want to be defined by my tragedies in his eyes.

There were, of course, advantages to revealing my life story. Unloading my personal information brought our conversation to a comfortable, real level. Intimate, without artifice. There was an easy ebb and flow between the humorous and the serious in our conversation. I felt like I was talking with someone from my own wonderful, dysfunctional family. It felt familiar. In some ways, I felt like Allen was a male version of me—just a much better, funnier version.

Allen would often stop midsentence to point out unique storefronts and irony. "That's convenient. A divorce attorney. Right next door to the shop where you can buy a wedding ring."

The comedy show wasn't nearly as fun as Allen. After all, the performance was free, since the comics were just trying out their material. Allen and I sat in the back and laughed at our own banter. Somehow, being around him filled me with loud, joyful laughter.

As I sat on the subway heading home, I realized I was laughing out loud as I recalled my evening. Just thinking about Allen brought a smile to my face. I felt reassured, as though my secret-sharing wasn't a deal breaker in our night. It was just another great moment we spent getting to know each other.

Some people ask me of my dates, "How do you choose? Who do you like the most?"

The truth is, each man is unique and charming in his own way. Even if I'm coming off a date with someone who's left me breathless, when I'm with that new man the next day, I do my best to be in the moment and try and pay attention to who *he* truly is. I'm learning that when I do that, it's much easier to appreciate whomever I'm with. And it's easier to be myself— even if that means revealing the loaded reality of my past. My worries fade, and the more caring, authentic, and appreciative side of me rises to the surface. And that makes me feel a little less crazy—about my life, this project, and the beautiful but complicated world of romance.

DATE 9: JON

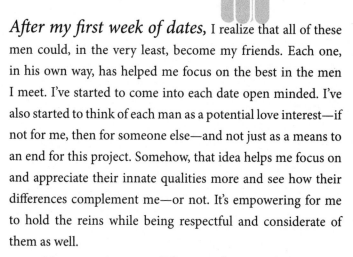

After my first week of dates, I realize that all of these men could, in the very least, become my friends. Each one, in his own way, has helped me focus on the best in the men I meet. I've started to come into each date open minded. I've also started to think of each man as a potential love interest—if not for me, then for someone else—and not just as a means to an end for this project. Somehow, that idea helps me focus on and appreciate their innate qualities more and see how their differences complement me—or not. It's empowering for me to hold the reins while being respectful and considerate of them as well.

My approach was no different with my ninth date.

At first glance, I wasn't sure what to think of Jon. Before we met, about all I knew was that he made films for fun and was a counselor of some sort. In person, he's a giant, quirky, artsy fellow with a devilishly fun nature and a poofy, dark-brown afro like Andre the Giant's. He'd blend in easily at a comic-book convention. He showed up for our date wearing a retro salmon jacket that he proudly admitted he'd snagged at the Salvation Army, and pointed out that it was a detour from his usual outfit: T-shirt, pajama bottoms, and a trench coat.

To my great relief, he was *not* in pajamas today.

If I had to distill him down to a collage of personas, I'd say he's a mix of mad scientist with a split personality shared by Santa Claus and the Cheshire Cat. I quickly figured him out: "You're twisted!" I said with delight.

I meant it as a compliment.

He laughed, proudly, it seemed.

We kicked off our day at the carousel in Central Park, which costs a mere $2. Jon brought out the kid in me. We pretended we were riding real horses, that we were flying or on a scary roller coaster. Sure, I felt silly—a little self-conscious (it's not easy letting go of your inhibitions)—but I had fun all the same.

For Jon, Central Park was a smorgasbord for the senses. I enjoyed seeing how much he loved it: the trees, the artists who sat painting canvases of park benches and ponds, the entertainers playing steel drums and singing. I'd somehow written Central Park off as a been-there-done-that kind of place, but experiencing it vicariously through Jon made me appreciate its vibrancy anew.

We moved from the park to another inner-child-friendly place: F.A.O. Schwarz, the city's iconic toy store.

We were welcomed by a man dressed as a toy soldier, who opened the towering doors for us, directing us into a magical world where Oz-like music blared overhead. Remote-control airplanes raced through the air and stuffed animals cozily piled together from floor to ceiling. Jon beamed, clearly in his element, and marched right up to what appeared to be his twin— a nine-foot-tall Lego statue of Hagrid, the giant magician from the Harry Potter stories. The replica even wore a bushy black beard and wig and a dark tan duster. Jon stood by Hagrid's side with pride, and the resemblance was striking. "If only I had an awesome beard like his!"

A man waved us over to his small kiosk, which was lined with Rubik's Cubes. He wore a name tag that read HECTOR and a headset with a microphone so that his next challenge could be heard by everyone near the front of the store. He grabbed a cube and eyed Jon.

"You mix it, I'll fix it," dared Hector, handing him the cube.

Jon handed the cube back. "*You* mix it and *I'll* fix it."

Hector smiled at the challenge. "Deal." As he twisted and turned the Rubik's to remix the colors, he explained the toy to the curious kids standing nearby. "You see, there are six different-colored sides and each side has nine blocks. But here I can rotate the sides around so that all the colors get mixed up. The challenge is to get them all back together, so that all the same colors get back to the same side."

I was just as curious to know its secrets and listened just as intently. You see, when I was a kid I could never figure out this toy. Not ever. I would get one or two sides all the same color, but then I'd just get frustrated and cheat. I would peel off the stickers and place all the red ones on the same side, all the blues together, the rest in their proper places, and would declare victory. Of course, no one believed I had actually solved the puzzle—probably because all the stickers were crooked or ripped!

Hector's cube started to look a little bit like my life: scrambled. I felt like I was trying to solve my own Rubik's Cube—one built of the nuances of dating and relationships. Hopefully, by the end of this project, I'd be better equipped to solve all its sides.

When Hector completed his quick-handed twists, he gave the cube to Jon. "Okay, big guy, let's see how quickly it takes you." Hector looked at his watch and started punching a few buttons. "On your mark, get set, *go!*"

Jon assessed the mess in his hands and started tackling his cubed opponent with rippling turns. Hector nodded in approval. "Oh, I see what you're doing there," he said. "He's going with the white cross technique," he told the growing crowd. "There are really only a few techniques to figure out the cube. And once you figure those out, it's not that hard to do the rest."

Jon whipped the cube around, showing that all nine white stickers now faced the same side. He kept working the other colors. He tapped at a red sticker, as if predicting where it would go next.

"You see," said Hector, "There's a circle in the middle and everything is linked to it. Once you figure out which side the colors go on, it's not too difficult to see where the rest fits."

Ah! So that's it. If I found my center, I'd have an easier time getting the rest of my life to fall into place. No pretending. I wouldn't know where to put the stickers, anyway.

Jon snapped the last color into place with pride, and Hector's thumb punched the button on his watch. "One minute, fifty-three seconds!" he announced. "Not bad!"

Jon shook his head in disappointment, "My time is usually *way* better than *that!*"

As we spent the next few hours in the store, that cube kept lingering in the back of my head. *What kind of person spends their time figuring that thing out?*

Jon and I painted with watercolors, threw bouncy balls around with kids, tapped out "Hot Cross Buns" on the store's famous pool-size floor piano. I even happily threw myself into a fluffy mass of pillows that looked like Strawberry Shortcake, while Jon went off to have a conversation with a puppet.

Jon and I are clearly different. He's twice as tall as I am and twice as zany. Honestly, before this project, I probably wouldn't have gone out on a date with him. I would have judged him quickly, somehow found flaws in his bushy hair, towering physique, and quirky demeanor. Within seconds, I would have developed a narrow first impression of him and decided that he wasn't for me. I can just imagine my justification: *Why go out with him when I know I'm not going to end up dating him? Why waste my time?* And then I'd imagine what my friends might say: "Really, Tamara? *Really?*"

But I did go out with him, and I'm *glad* I did. While Jon may not be someone I would typically date, he's nonetheless an incredible person, with depth, intelligence, warmth, and good humor. He might not appear to be *my* ideal, but I can easily see his allure to others. And being around him is humbling. In those few hours getting to know him and his life story, I developed a sense of humility, a trait that can sometimes get lost in a self-centered world where "me me me" trumps the consideration of others.

You see, Jon's job is to help children with autism, a disorder that has impacted him and his family almost his entire life.

Jon was ten years old when his youngest brother was diagnosed with autism. His relationship with his brother helped him become a more compassionate and creative person. He always lived outside the box.

I get now how Jon could figure out that pesky Rubik's Cube.

There are millions of ways that six-sided cube can be twisted, and there are only a handful of techniques to get all the same-colored stickers on one side. All that's required is patience and maybe even a little thinking outside the box.

The same goes for me and dating. Instead of assuming a guy is a waste of my time, I need to keep setting aside my pride, expect the unexpected, and invest a little more time.

I might just match up my sides.

DATE 10: BILLY

I've been hearing from a lot of guys lately who don't necessarily want to be part of the project but are still supportive. I feel like more men get that I'm not doing this project to trash men, I'm simply trying to figure out how to take control of my own romantic intentions and learn to discern real potential from wish making when it comes to the men I date. Because the latter has not served me well—I just end up with unreal expectations and a bruised heart.

Guys who were friends of mine in college are revealing how they wish they had had the courage to ask me out all those years ago. A few men I've dated casually have said they thought we should have been more serious. A couple days ago, I even received an email from You Know Who—that photographer from Boston who *almost* broke up with me on the way to the airport.

His email was quintessentially him, poetic and totally confusing. I wasn't sure if it was a case of his fondly remembering the good times and wanting to reattempt a relationship or if it was just some FYI afterthought. *By the way, despite how cold I was to you when we broke up, I still feel love for you. Just wanted to let you know! Hey, let's keep in touch! Hope we can be friends.*

Of course, that's not what he wrote, but it's certainly how it came across.

I wrote him back a short note:

"Thanks for writing. I'm actually pretty busy right now seeing a couple dozen other guys, but it would be great to catch up when I'm done with the project! Hope you're doing well."

As far as the guys who've participated in the project, I've been trying to keep in contact as best as I can. But I'm pretty much leaving the ball in their court. I figure if they're interested in anything more, then they'll reach out. Which is a big departure for me. I am usually the pursuer in relationships—and too often relentlessly so. This was good practice.

I keep hearing from Ryan (Date 4, Harlem gospel guy), who checks up on me with friendly banter. (A few of my girl-friends have cyber-crushes on him now.) Chris (Date 3, Knicks game), Joel (Date 2, Brooklyn Bridge boy), and Adam (Date 5, all-day date) keep me updated on how they're doing. Mostly I've been keeping in touch with Evan (Date 6, the surfer who bailed me out last-minute). We keep our online chats light and brief, mostly saying hello and sharing small talk. All have been really kind and understand that not only am I busy with work and the project, but I'm also tired, running on an average of four or five hours of sleep every night, and struggling to fill my calendar.

A few days ago I widened my search for men by signing up with a free, local dating site. But most of the guys pretty much creeped me out.

Immediately after I registered a username, messages streamed across my screen like verbal pop-up porn. "Hey Sexy, wuss up?" "How U Doin?" "We should meet." "Send me your pix!"

Those few notes made me cringe, which is why I was caught off guard when I received this email:

> Hello Tamara,
>
> My name is Billy and I found your list of Rules on the Craigslist "platonic only" section.

Craigslist? Who had posted my Rules on Craigslist?

I hopped online, searched the site, and in a few seconds saw my "Rules" staring back at me, with my name and email address listed.

Panic set in. After my creepy online experience, I didn't want a bunch of men seeking me out for an Internet love affair, even if it were just for a day.

But Billy seemed like a normal guy. He offered references. He linked me to some of his online profile pages, and he even left me the names and numbers of some of his friends. *Nice.*

I had never been on a true "blind date" before. So far in the project, even the men I hadn't met before the date were at least friends of friends. I'd never met up with a complete stranger before. I was a tad nervous about it.

We decided to meet in Battery Park and take the ferry to the Statue of Liberty and Ellis Island. I was pleasantly surprised when I saw the handsome Asian guy walk up to me. He looked normal—dressed in jeans and a warm coat, which he held on to tightly for warmth, if not for protection from our unusual meeting. He was well kempt and had a shy smile. "Billy?" I asked. It was him. And he was anything but creepy. Maybe just a little nervous.

It was cold out, and the frigid air made for smaller crowds and shorter lines. We sat on the ferry and talked about our typical dating habits, and I asked him why he had contacted me. "I wanted to try something new," he said. I could totally relate.

As the boat cut through the icy water, we made small talk. He seemed smart and grounded, but I felt a little awkward in his presence. I couldn't quite be my open self.

We stepped onto Liberty Island and I gazed up at the green lady. Close up, she gave me a feeling of strength and possibility. For years in my dating life I'd felt much like her, shouting to single men everywhere, "Give me your tired, your poor!" My whole dating life had felt like one giant huddled mass of men who looked at me as a gateway, their ticket to becoming someone else's husband. But today the statue held different meaning for me, offering me freedom from my past mistakes and a new dating life paved with gold.

Billy and I toured the base of the monument, which was a small museum dedicated to the statue's history. I had forgotten the delicate work the French had put into Lady Liberty's creation, and the sacrifices that had been made to bring the sixty thousand pounds of metal to our nation.

We headed into the stairwell and I felt a knot in my stomach looking up at the 354 empty steps leading to her crown.

"I'm a little afraid of heights," I mentioned, feeling vertigo as we hiked upstairs.

It was clear he didn't know quite what to do about it.

"Um, do you want to stop?" he asked.

"No, no, I'll be okay. I'm into taking risks these days."

He said okay, and I felt self-conscious as I mentally psyched myself into carefully walking up the steps. *You're safe. You're doing great. This is totally worth it.*

We walked up just high enough to see Manhattan from one of the windows along the seemingly endless staircase. I asked Billy questions about himself, hoping to fill the space with his stories and distract me from my fear.

He was born in China and immigrated to the United States with his family when he was only six years old. He arrived in New York City speaking Cantonese and Taishanese.

"Taishanese?" I asked. "Never heard of that one before."

"What can I say? I'm not like every other guy," he said with a timid smile. It was the first time I felt like I started to see him loosen up a little.

"So here I was," he said, "in New York, speaking languages no one else spoke. So I had to teach myself English."

"You taught your*self?*" I blurted out, suddenly impressed out of my stupor of fear.

"Yeah, but it wasn't as hard as it seems. I was a kid. Went to school. Watched television. I figured it out."

"Well, no wonder you're a self-made man."

On the boat ride over, I learned that Billy studied economics at NYU, but as soon as he entered the world of stocks, he realized he wanted to do something else. So he taught himself how to create websites and started his own company. For fun, he played poker. He even taught himself the tricks of the game and developed his own style and techniques to win. I was impressed by his tenacity and discipline. Still, something felt off. We were total opposites. He seemed quiet and reserved and I was loud and unabashed. I wasn't sure we had a lot in common, but I tried to remind myself of my unspoken dating rule: to make the best of it—and him.

I focused on where we were going next and felt a surge of excitement. *Ellis Island.*

When I was a kid, I remember visiting the Statue of Liberty and pointing curiously to the large, black, dilapidated mass across the way. For years, Ellis Island stood ignored in the shadow of Lady Liberty, and only since the 1980s have millions of dollars been poured into its restoration. These days, it's beautiful.

As we headed toward the main building, I started skipping. "I hope you like it here." I said to Billy, "because I *love* Ellis Island." I felt myself loosening up as I stepped onto familiar ground.

"I've never been here, but it looks cool so far," he said.

"You've gotta understand," I told him, "*this* is the spot where my father's family first arrived when they came from

Slovakia a hundred years ago!" My excitement enlivened me, and I lectured excitedly about the details. "Apparently they would all get these colored badges to wear, and each color signified what language the person spoke or what city they were headed to. All of our family went to Cleveland. Except for one uncle, who apparently was put on the wrong bus and made his way to Chicago instead."

Billy smiled as he listened. He seemed amused by my enthusiasm.

I continued my talking tour, taking him into the Grand Hall, where millions of immigrants had stood, waiting to make their way into the country. I felt the energy of my forefathers and felt gratitude for the steps my family had taken to get here. It made me realize the challenges Billy faced in his own life to become the man he is today—as shy as he seems, he's brave enough to email a random girl and ask her out on a date. Even with our different personalities, the fact that Billy and I shared an immigrant history—like all Americans—made me feel a closer affinity to him. We were even sharing the experience of crossing into a "new world" of dating together. We had both begun the day a little scared of something and someone new. But despite all our differences, we had become friends in our handful of hours together.

DATE 11:
JASON

"I'm not very good at verbal communication," he wrote. "I'm much better with communicating physically."
Wait . . . WHAT? Didn't you read my rules?!

That should have been my first indication that Jason would be a much different date than all the other men . . .

I met him for dessert at one of New York's classic East Side spots, Serendipity III. I was struck by his sophisticated good looks, his close-cropped black hair, and his chiseled Asian features. But I could immediately tell he was a "shy guy." He had a big nervous smile as he shifted toward me, hugging me hello. He then reached down to pick up a giant bouquet of pink roses he had stashed by his feet. "These are for you," he said.

I searched for the right words as I tried to hide my expression of surprise. *A dozen roses? On a first date? With someone you've never met?*

"These are beautiful," I said, swallowing back my own sudden nervousness. "Thank you. You *really* shouldn't have . . . "

"I wanted to get you something special," he said, "because *you're* special."

Okay. Let's just freeze here for a minute. Yes, I, too, was wondering whether this guy was just old fashioned, naive, or supersuave.

The little angel and devil Tamaras that sat on my shoulders bickered about it.

Devil [*rolling her eyes*]: *Is this guy seriously trying to win you over with this stuff?*

Angel: *Be nice! He's just an old-fashioned gentleman. It's thoughtful.*

I tried my best to shut them down, but I had a feeling this conflict would continue throughout the evening.

As we dove into our shared dessert, it was clear that Jason was true-blue about one thing: He's not much for words. When he does speak his voice quivers, and he laughs as if he's unsure about what he's saying. His quiet personality aligns with all of his interests, which require little verbal communication. He travels abroad to record and edit videos, he ice skates, he even graduated high school early, leaving its highly social environment to study accounting. What I found most fascinating about him was his dancing, an interest that seemed so counter to his personality, and something he'd been doing all his life.

He opened up more as I asked him about it. I learned that when he was a child, he danced with one of the top ballet troupes in New York. And now—talk about schisms—he teaches the Argentine tango, which is what he planned to teach me.

As we walked down the street to the dance hall, Jason was already applauding my technique. "See?" he said. "You're already learning the first steps to tango! If you can walk, you can tango."

He gently linked my arm with his. As he spoke about dance, his voice became more confident. "The most important part of the tango is getting close to your partner."

Uh-oh.

We arrived at the tango bar, which was a tight space with low lighting and loud instrumental music piping overhead. A group of fancy-dressed people cheered upon Jason's entry. "Where have you *been?*" they asked.

"I'm sorry," he explained, "I've been filming in South Africa."

An older woman with big curly red hair and a feather boa bounced over to me. "Helloooo!" she said. "I'm Betty! Do *you* tango *too?*"

"Oh, no," I explained. "This is my first time."

"Oh, you will *love* the tango," she insisted. "It sweeps your heart away on the dance floor."

Her partner—an older man wearing a suit and a flower on his lapel—nudged his way toward me. "Did I hear correctly? This is your *first time* with the tango? Well, you will simply *love* it."

"Thank you," I said, suddenly feeling underdressed and underprepared for whatever was ahead.

"I'm Fred," he said, reaching for my hand.

"Tamara," I said, as he cupped my hand and kissed my knuckle.

"It's a pleasure to meet you, Tamara," he said. "I've been dancing the tango for over fifty years. It's the secret to my long life. Guess how old I am."

"How *old?*" I'm never quite sure how to answer this question without offending someone.

"Ninety years old!" he said proudly. "And not a *day* goes by that I don't think about the tango." And then he leaned in closely as if to tell me a secret. "You know," he said, "many people believe that the tango is just the first step to foreplay."

Hmmm. In that case, I'd be sure to avoid dancing with *him* tonight.

I gently let go of Fred's hand, hoping the dark lighting made it difficult for him to see the uncomfortable look on my face. "Well, thank you for the warning."

Jason grabbed my other hand and led me to the back room, where two couples swayed closely on a dimly lit dance floor. My heart raced and my stomach turned as I realized that Jason would soon be nuzzled close to me. Dancing was definitely taking me out of my comfort zone. But I was game. This was what it was all about, right?

Jason led me to the back of the room and talked me through the basics. He spoke with authority for the first time that evening. "There are a few steps you'll need to remember." He raised his head and arms and started to move as if he were with an imaginary partner. "Slow . . . slow. Quick-quick."

He was clearly an amazing dancer, and I suddenly felt a little intimidated. I took a tiny step back with my right foot, then left. Right. Left. I nodded to Jason as if I understood his instruction.

"You ready?"

I nodded again. Somehow I had become the silent one.

Jason came toward me and stood confidently in my presence. His face was so close that I could hear him breathe. "Now," he whispered, "we'll just take a few minutes to get comfortable with one another. The most important part of tango is to feel comfortable with your partner. So let's sway a bit."

Did I feel comfortable with him? I wasn't sure. The physical closeness was so sudden and intimate. Jason was certainly a nice guy, but my feelings for him weren't really in line with the sensual energy of tango.

Well, here goes . . .

He took his hands and placed them gently on my hips, leaning into me. My arms lifted to his shoulders, hesitantly hugging him. We moved slowly side to side, and I could feel my pulse begin to pound intensely. His proximity made me a little nervous. I barely knew him, and here we were, our bodies pressed together. I was feeling more awkward than my two left feet as I stumbled around the floor with him, trying to get my bearings.

Just enjoy the dance, I told myself. *Take advantage of the free lesson.*

I felt his hand push slightly on my hip as he stepped with his left leg, forcing my leg to follow his stride.

He whispered the steps to me, "Slow . . . slow . . . quick, quick. Just follow me and you'll know tango in no time."

He kept his hands guiding my hips as I tripped through his instructions. My muscles tightened, resisting his lead.

He stopped to help me regain focus. "You're doing great so far. Just relax. Tango has more to do with trusting yourself and your partner than anything," he said, smiling. "I won't let you mess up."

I tried to focus more on his encouragement and training tips and less on the persistence of his body heat.

Okay, self. Get over it, already.

I took a deep breath. He took my right arm in his hand and guided me once again with gliding, delicate sweeping steps. My leg drifted on the floor, my back held strong, and I started to feel the beauty of the tango.

Slow . . . slow . . . quick, quick.

Slow . . . slow . . . quick, quick.

The rhythm began to feel less scary, more automatic. Just as everyone had promised, I was starting to *love* the tango.

Jason guided me across the room, my footsteps in sync with the flowing music. He pulled my hips to his and we walked close together. His breath tickled the edge of my ear. *Oh crap!* I sensed his desire, and my heart pounded faster. Don't get me wrong, I'm no prude, but I simply wasn't attracted to Jason, and I began to feel like I was losing control of where we were heading on this date. Jason turned his head and I could feel him staring at me, considering his next move.

Please don't try to kiss me! Please please please . . .

But he was going to anyway. I could sense it coming from a mile away—or, in our case, an eighth of an inch away. He slowed his dance, stood still, and gently swept his lips across mine. I instinctively turned my head away and stepped back.

I could feel my heart racing. I kept swaying away from him, turning my face as far away from his as possible.

He kept stopping, pulled me in again, and then kissed me on the mouth. Slow . . . slow, quick.

Um, excuse me, tango boy, didn't you read my dating rules? Remember how I said the dates would be G rated? Since when did Snow White *include the passionate kisses on the dance floor? No tongue tango, please.*

I realized then that it was my responsibility to be clear about my boundaries. For all I knew, he'd been misreading my signals—I decided to give him the benefit of the doubt.

"Jason," I said pulling my head back and pushing away from him, "let's just dance, okay? Kissing isn't really on the dessert menu tonight." I held his gaze. "I appreciate it."

He looked surprised, even a little abashed, but nodded. "Okay, sure. Sorry." He laughed, a little embarrassed, it seemed.

Devil: *You were too easy on him!*

Angel [*winking*]: *Au contraire. You were an angel.*

Okay. I felt a little more in control now. I let him take me close once again. Every now and then I would feel his face turn toward mine—but I held firm. And I was proud of how I handled it. I'd found myself in an uncomfortable entanglement, and I'd spoken up, set my boundaries.

Even though he was directing me around the dance floor, I was finally directing the dynamics of the date. As for the tango, maybe I'd wait on a second lesson.

DATE 12: CHRISTIAN

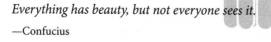

Everything has beauty, but not everyone sees it.
—Confucius

For the last few days, my coworkers have been hounding me, saying my project would be the "perfect" story for our show *Good Morning America.* But the suggestion of appearing on national television to talk about how I turned my disastrous dating life into a project makes me about as nervous as the thought of walking around New York City naked.

"Tam," they insist, "you *have* to tell Diane about it."

Diane. As in *Diane Sawyer.* The queen of television news.

I'm okay with my friends and family reading about my latest dating adventure—I'm even okay with a bunch of unidentified voyeurs. But the thought of talking about it to the newswoman I admire and respect most—much less blathering to the entire nation—is more attention (and possible criticism) than I can handle right now. My self-criticism is cruel enough as it is.

With my friends' constant urging, I nervously attempted to write her an email:

~~Dear Diane. Hey Diane.~~ Diane,

Some of the producers ~~have been bugging me about~~ suggested telling you about ~~this dumb idea I have~~ a little project I'm doing during my off-hours. It might sound silly but . . .

I provided her with the brief details of my project and waited a few days before pressing "send."

The growing pressure of this project and my decreasing hours of sleep are making me surly . . . and probably not the best person to be out with on a date. At least, that's how I felt as I rushed to meet Christian the comedian. I was twenty minutes late—and completely frazzled. Our date fell during the Chinese New Year celebration, so we planned to follow the parade as it weaved through Chinatown. I couldn't help but note my affinity with the year's animal: the ox. People born during the Year of the Ox are hardworking, goal-oriented, patient, focused, and tenacious—even when tired. Through its dedication, the ox prospers—or so it's said. If I could keep working at being less vulnerable, avoiding quick judgments, being my best and most true self, and treating myself and these men with respect, I believe I will somehow prosper.

I found myself in total work mode, with the focused gaze of a kid playing video games as I rushed through the streets trying to meet Christian, dodging any obstacle thrown my way. I got lost trying to reach our meeting spot and found myself wandering along the zigzag streets of Chinatown, which are confusing. They're outlined as if a cartographer dropped a bowl of chow mein on a table and decided the noodley mess would suffice as a proper map. I tried to mentally navigate my journey, rushing to meet him while attempting to keep my cool and juggle the boatloads of other thoughts in my head: my flubs with Jason the night before, my work schedule for the week, the boys I've liked already, laundry . . .

Every few minutes, I updated Christian on my whereabouts via a stream of frenetic-sounding texts: "5 minutes away!" "Almost there!" "So sorry! Please forgive me!!!"

Every time I saw his name in my inbox, I smiled with delight, knowing I was about to get a good laugh. Of course he had the upper hand with humor: He's a professional comedian who teaches improvisation, which is a great outlet for his goofy, clever, sarcastic sense of humor. He sent me a text back. "Take your time. I just joined the Joy Luck Club and am getting beat at mah-jongg by a woman who looks like she was alive during the Ming Dynasty." *What if he turns out to be another guy I find myself really liking?*

I turned the corner, breathless, and finally caught a glimpse of Christian, standing patiently by a big statue of Confucius, the ancient Chinese philosopher whose wisdom still hides in fortune cookies. He waved, recognizing me, and smiled a toothy grin. He was tall with a wave of short, dark hair. For some reason I think I expected him to look like a comedian, although I was not sure what that meant. After all, I wouldn't have been too charmed by a guy wearing a squirting flower on his lapel instead of Christian's everyday garb of jeans and a T-shirt with a puffy ski jacket.

"I'm sorry for being late," I heaved, still breathing heavily from my sprint to find him. I gave him a guilty look and a quick hug hello.

"No problem," he said good-naturedly.

I found myself feeling platonic and guarded, with no time to debate whether I had any initial attraction to him. I ditched the moments typically meant for small-talk introductions, pushing forward as if at work, still focused on our goal for the day.

"The parade is just a few blocks away," he said. "You wanna try to catch up with it? Or we can stay here for a bit so you can catch your breath."

Thoughtful, patient guy. Nice.

"No, no," I insisted. "Let's try to catch up. Besides," I added, smiling, "I'm already warmed up."

We hustled along the street, following the sound of loud drums that beat a joyous cadence through the streets. Colorful confetti littered the recently abandoned sidewalk, and, much like bread crumbs, we followed them to the heart of the parade.

Hundreds of people crowded together, cheering and skipping down the streets, as they followed the progress of the parade. Guiding it along were a riot of intricately designed green, red, and gold lion masks, which bobbed and weaved atop the shoulders of teenage boys who danced in sync to the drums to ward off evil spirits. Christian and I kept getting separated as we were corralled by revelers. I was thrust into the wave rushing up the street, bumped and jostled by people who shouted joyously in Chinese. I felt like a foreigner in my own city. Even claustrophobic. I squelched a stirring of panic as I eyed the crowd for Christian.

And there he was, in a pack of people nearby, three deep away from me. He caught my eye and pointed down the street, mouthing the words "You wanna go?" I nodded, relieved, and wiggled my way past the partiers and away from the celebration.

The cacophony of the parade faded as we walked into a little shop called Rice to Riches, a sleek, pastel, futuristic-looking place that makes unique rice pudding concoctions with chocolate chips, or cookies and cream, or graham crackers. Christian seemed uncertain about the menu. "French toast–flavored pudding?" he asked with a grimace.

"We can go somewhere else," I said, "but I've heard this place is good." Really, though, I wanted to finally just *sit still,* so we'd have a chance to talk and I could rest my feet. So far, his kindness and good humor were positive signs. *He's a genuinely nice guy,* I thought, relieved.

"This is fine," he said. "I'm just glad I no longer feel like I'm running with the bulls." I laughed, totally relating.

We decided on our dishes—vanilla for him, almond for me—and then slipped into a nearby booth with pink vinyl seats.

Christian settled in with a look of relief. "I just wanted us to go somewhere we could sit and talk, and where I can actually look you in the eye," he says, laughing, gesturing from his eyes to mine.

I was so glad we were in alignment. I was exhausted, still feeling restless and needing to relax a little. It was reassuring to know that he was as interested in getting to know me as I was him. It made for a level playing field—but I still felt a little distracted and guarded.

I shook the confetti out of my hair and took a bite of the pudding, enjoying the soft texture. Christian dominated the conversation, sharing funny stories in between small, polite spoonfuls of his own pudding.

Despite stories of his clowning, I learned that he's also a deeply intelligent and socially aware man as well: a scholar who studied at top schools for undergrad and Harvard for grad school, and then did a teaching stint at MIT for postgraduate work. He's helped develop educational strategies for underprivileged children as well, but amid all his brilliance, he admitted to a history mixed with greatness and great blunders. He believed himself a bit of a buffoon. I listened, but I felt a little like it was an interview I was conducting, and I wanted to shake the feeling like I did the confetti. But it lingered.

"I just don't think I've ever really *gotten it*," he said, looking suddenly thoughtful.

"It?" I said, surprised. His sudden, unexpected candor jolted me, and I felt myself shifting toward Tamara-the-*person* he was on a date with, not Tamara-the-serial-dater checking off another date.

"Yeah. Like, figuring out how to act around people. I always end up doing exactly what no normal person would do in a social situation. Like the time I won a costume contest in the sixth grade. That's supposed to be a moment of glory, right? The whole class turned to cheer for me," he said, raising his arms in victory, "and I was *so embarrassed*. Everyone was looking at me. So I bolted out the door and into the hall-way. The teachers had no idea what was wrong. They started chasing me down the hall. And I headed straight for the boys' room to hide."

"Awww, Christian," I said, feeling more playful, "you were the weird kid. How sweet."

"Weird *and* clueless," he said, laughing.

"Then there was the time I was racing to the door in junior high. That was back when they had that glass in the doors with all the crisscrossed wire in it—"

"Oh, yeah. That scary-looking glass."

"Yep. *Safety* glass was what they called it. So I'm running toward the door—*again* running away from everyone—and I smash my hand through the glass."

"Ouch!" I cringed in empathy and instinctively grabbed my own hand. "Were you okay? I mean, I *see* you're okay, but . . . "

He pulled back his long sleeve and showed me a small scar running from the base of his hand to his wrist. "Battle wound," he said proudly.

"But that isn't anywhere near as bad as what I did in high school," he added, laughing as if he were amused by his own embarrassment. He turned over his hand to show another series of long, threaded scars by his wrist.

"I was playing basketball in PE and someone passed me the ball and my hand just *shattered.*"

"What do you mean, it *just shattered?*"

"I really have no idea what happened. But the bones broke so badly that I had to wear one of those *L*-shaped casts," he said, raising his arm to a ninety-degree angle, "All *senior year.*"

I burst into uncontrollable laughter, mixed with guilty apologies. "I'm so sorry!" I giggled. "That's *so awful*. But *so funny*." Tears streamed from my eyes. "This is *really* your life?" As we tried to compose ourselves, I felt like I was an audience member watching him perform—but it didn't feel like he was performing, which was good. I wanted our connection to be authentic, and I felt like *I* was the one who needed to relax and be myself a little more. His humor was doing a good job at breaking down my walls.

"I needed that laugh," I sighed loudly, trying to calm my laughter. "Whoo. I *needed* that. I feel like I've been all wound up since rushing to meet you."

"Well . . . " he said, as he stared down at his ricey-cinnamon dish, "you definitely look like a girl who's been going out on a lot of dates."

And there it is.

"Oh no!" I exclaimed in embarrassment. "I'm so sorry."

"It's okay. It just seems like you're in a 'work mindset.' Like you were on a mission. I thought, *This girl's definitely been going out on dates for the last two weeks.*"

His words struck me hard, because I realized that while I was trying to get to know him, I was nonetheless doing it in the context of the "dating project," which kind of made the endeavor more self-serving than a traditional date. That's the catch-22 here, I guess, and a great reminder to be more aware of my *own* authenticity.

"It's just that I felt like over email we had this really good thing going on," he said, gesturing his hands back and forth as if he were pulling the two of us together. "And then you show up and I was just confused. I thought, *Hello! Wake up!*"

He was right. Over email I was nearly smitten by him. But as soon as I met him, I locked up and felt guarded. I was thinking about how late I was. I was still disconcerted about kissing Jason. I was wondering about the other guys who had already tugged on my heartstrings. And I wasn't sure whether I would end up being attracted to Christian. I was holding back and he was calling me on it.

I shook my head in apology, embarrassed. "I really wasn't totally there, was I?"

I realized then that there's a pattern that's been developing with each of these dates. When I first contact each guy, I get a feel for his personality and make a guess about "where things could go" based on our online conversations. Before the dating project, I would have held on to that feeling and it would have dictated my behavior throughout the rest of the date. For instance, if I had thought, *This guy is just going to be my friend,* then I would have acted like just a friend. Same goes for the thought, *I totally want to marry this guy.* I would have then put on my best "cool girl" act and hoped he saw me as a potential partner. Dating every day has brought these self-limiting habits to my attention.

I've been trying just to roll with things, let go of my pre-judgments, and see what happens. When I do that, there is typically a second or third moment of reassessment that offers a more real, solid understanding of who the guy is and what our future could hold. In Christian's case, I had originally thought he was hilarious and I wanted to get to know him better. Then we met in person, and there was a disconnect.

Maybe I expected to be more attracted to him, physically, up front. Maybe it was dating fatigue, or fallout from the previous night's date, or sleep deprivation, or . . . there were so many variables! And then when we did have the chance to sit down and talk, I felt a little like he was performing, and he thought I was guarded. We were not on a level field, after all. It took his calling me on it to rebalance the potential of the date, and it took his stepping out from behind his comedian persona, too. We reached a place where we both became more honest and open. Not only that, we both seemed to cross into that zone of vulnerability, that moment where—at least for me—I go from feeling it's a "no risk first date" to being in "I hope this person likes me" mode.

The New Year's celebration had subsided. The drums were gone. The dragons and the crowds had scattered. Maybe those age-old traditions really worked. Maybe they really did ward off evil spirits. Maybe they really did set the stage for something new.

I said a warm goodbye to Christian, feeling good about our day, and when I got home I discovered an email in my inbox that set my heart beating in double time:

It's from Diane Sawyer—friendly, warm. She liked my project and wanted me to appear on our show. She thought it would be fun to mention around Valentine's Day. I was now totally a nervous wreck.

Apparently, the Year of the Ox was officially here.

DATE 13: MICHAEL

You'd think that having a date every day would ease my feelings of nervousness, but as I headed downtown to meet Michael for some hummus and rock music, I was hit by an immense wave of insecurity. *What if we don't get along?* I thought. *What if he thinks I'm boring?* I took a deep, body-filling breath and tried to relieve the tension in my shoulders and back.

Originally, Michael had been Date 6, which was the one where I went and saw *A Really Bad Play*. But lest you think he was some guy flaking out on me, it wasn't his fault at all. I realized too late that the play started an hour earlier than I'd assumed (since when does a curtain rise at seven o'clock?), and he simply couldn't get out of class before the play began. Considering it was a medical school course he'd have to ditch, I didn't begrudge his staying in school for the night, so we postponed until tonight (as you may recall, I met Evan for the play instead—an unexpected bonus date who still makes me giddy).

So here we were, Date 13, and while I'm not superstitious (okay, maybe a little "'stitious"), my brain was trying to force connections between that loaded number and the ironic circumstances and timing. A few days before, I was startled to see him across the room at a wedding reception, and—like a bride and groom just before their nuptials—we purposely avoided each other, catching eyes now and again. Later, he admitted that he didn't even check out my website or Internet profile before we went out because he didn't want to come into the date with any preconceived impressions of me.

I wasn't sure how much we might have in common, other than having mutual friends who kept suggesting he accompany me on one of my thirty-one dates.

After all, he was the absolute cliché of the handsome, young, single doctor (to be).

That can be a little intimidating, but he was much more easygoing and down to earth than I expected—not an uptight, condescending smarty-pants—which was refreshing. He suggested we meet for hummus downtown before checking out some live music. As we met, I realized the music might be the most noise I'd hear for the night, as Michael turned out to be the quiet, cerebral type. He was tall and thin, with swirling brown locks of hair drooping softly onto his brow. He walked toward me outside The Hummus Place with his head down and shoulders in, probably deep in thought about something or just supporting the weight of the heavy backpack he carried.

"Hi, Michael," I said warily, hoping to avoid interrupting an important thought.

"Oh, hi!" he brightened, as if I'd caught him off guard. His smile crept slightly onto his face, and that's when I noticed his dark brown eyes, perfectly framed by a pair of classic black-rimmed eyeglasses. I'd like to think I'm not a superficial girl, but I have to admit, I liked Michael's look. His basic jeans-and-a-long-sleeve-T-shirt student uniform gave him that "I don't care what I look like" vibe, but without the contrived-cool factor. He looked like he was one of those bookish, NPR-listening, vegan hipster guys who's constantly analyzing the world and wondering how to improve it, which is definitely the type of person I love being around. Maybe he'd bring out my inner hippie.

He appeared enigmatic to me. Mysterious. And although he didn't walk with a confident strut, or offer me a forceful handshake, or talk loudly (if much at all), I could feel a sense of inner strength in him, but maybe with a hint of distraction. He was definitely a guy who was in his own head, consumed with big thoughts. For a smart guy, I'm not sure he's picked up on the fact that he's good-looking.

He opened the door for me, and we ordered some hummus and falafel at the counter. "Do you eat meat?" I asked him, wondering if he really did live up to my hipster/vegan/liberal stereotype. He looked off to the side as he answered, "I try not to." Was he embarrassed? Maybe he wasn't as confident as I'd pegged him to be.

"Oh," I beamed. "Me either." Having an instant commonality boosted my confidence, which helped put me at ease. But in a way, I also found myself wishing I were even more like him.

Within a few minutes, I was delighted to learn about something else we had in common: Michael was also raised in the D.C. area. And just to add to the "we have *so* much in common" cliché, he even went to one of my rival high schools—the one attended by all the tech and science kids. That was the high school where kids traditionally got near-perfect scores on their SATs, patented their own inventions, and started rehearsing acceptance speeches for Nobel prizes and presidential nominations. Whereas for me at the crowded public school, filled with happily diversified kids from all around the world, from military brats to senators' daughters, socializing always trumped studying. I felt like I was fifteen again, wondering if I would be able to keep up with this cute, brilliant boy. I wasn't so much intimidated as I was inspired to prove myself wrong.

We sat quietly, eating falafel. I tried to guide the conversation, feeling a little like I was at work, interviewing someone who didn't like to talk much. I asked open-ended questions about his classes, but his short answers, like "It's all right" and "Today's class was tough," made me realize his head might still be stuck in the classroom. So I chalked it up to his meeting me on one of his less stellar days. Sometimes that happens. Like when I met Christian and was so overwhelmed and rushed, winding through Chinatown. I wasn't at my best. Maybe that's how Michael was tonight.

After finishing the last of our meal, we headed a few blocks to a pub to hear Peter Conway, a British bluesy rocker, who was offering a free midnight show. We sat down across from the bar, at a table that was draped with a big sheet of white paper. A plastic cup filled with well-used crayons sat in the center of the table. The lighting was just bright enough for us to see while we colored.

"So, what kind of medicine do you want to go into?" I asked.

"Eh," he shrugged, "I'm not really sure. I'm kind of thinking of taking a break to do something else."

"Oh yeah? To do what?"

That's when I discovered I was talking to someone who was not just a "brain" but a brain-*ologist*. Michael thinks medical school is "fun," but worries that it might not be enough of a challenge for him. Seriously. Instead, he's hoping to take a break to pursue a PhD in his real passion: neuroscience. I was totally intrigued. Neuroscience has always been one of those highfalutin fields I'd love to study—like oncology or intellectual property law—but I would never actually invest the years of school it takes to master. And here was a guy who was living the parallel life in academia I could only dream of.

Then he showed me his backpack, which contained three thick hardback scholarly books about the inner workings of the brain. Apparently, one can't have enough "light reading" when there's time to kill on the subway.

"Let me get this straight. You're thinking of dropping out of *med school*—to become a *neuroscientist?*" I asked, trying to wrap my head around each syllable.

Michael's somber expression seemed to light up. "The brain is *so cool*," he said, and he grabbed a green crayon out of the cup and began to scribble.

This was the first time I really saw Michael smile. Finally, he seemed relaxed.

"What is it that fascinates you about it?" I asked.

His eyes sparked with passion as he talked about the functions of the brain. "See, this is the brain stem," he said, drawing quick swirling lines that made sense only to him.

"And this little guy right here," he said, scribbling his crayon, "this almond-shaped bit, is called the amygdala."

"Oh, yeah, I've heard of that place," I said. "The fear place, right? I use my amygdala all the time," I said, smiling.

Michael went into detail about how it all works. "The fear center helps assess danger and releases cortisol, which can make a person tense up."

Yeah, I thought, *like I felt right before I met* you.

Apparently, that same fancy nugget in the brain is also one of the alarm zones for first impressions. Researchers say that within the first second or so of our meeting someone, our little amygdala responds to quick judgments, our "fight or flight" instincts might kick in, and our brain somehow holds on to the ideas we've formulated in a split second, waiting to be proven wrong. And I definitely get that aspect. I totally judge Michael and every guy I meet instantly, wondering if it's someone I can handle being around or if I need to head for the hills. I'm just trying to give those first impressions a chance, allowing them to give me a general idea of the guy, instead of making a finite prediction of whether the two of us will live happily ever after. *Dang you, amygdala, and your tricky ways!*

Michael also went into details—ones I didn't understand, but that intrigued me nonetheless—of his hypotheses about specific brain functions and his belief, based on his findings, that we can heal certain ailments, maybe even stuff like cancer.

Really? This guy has taken up *neuroscience* as a *hobby* and he already has hypotheses about how to save the world. My dating project started to seem self-indulgent and silly by comparison.

I started to realize that Michael is more than just a "brain." He's a poet personified. He's a dreamer. He's debating giving up his pursuit of a top-notch medical degree to take a risk pursuing his passions and his gut-feeling predictions about the brain. I saw beyond his silent demeanor and began to see him as an individual for who he truly was. I liked him. But I could tell he wasn't interested in me. I saw how much passion he had about the brain—none of that inner fire seemed to translate when we were talking about me. Which was fine. I liked him anyway.

All this talk about thinking had me thinking: *How much do I consult my brain when I'm dating? How often do I follow my heart and not my head? Is one more important than the other?*

I have often heard the wisdom "Love him with your heart and marry him with your head." Do I have the mental or emotional stamina to balance the two equally? It hasn't been so easy to walk away from someone I've loved, no matter how much he drove me crazy. My heart always gets carried away, easily swayed by men who are funny, or smart, or who wear cute glasses and talk neuroscience. Maybe it's time my brain started working a little more with my heart, constantly asking me not only if I like or respect the guy I'm with, but also if I feel fully comfortable with who I am while I'm with him.

I can feel myself growing out of those first-impression fears and feeling a little excited about meeting this handsome, brainy stranger. I loved being around Michael. I predict he will change the world, one curious thought at a time. He's inspiring, one of those guys who make me want to go home and start painting, enroll in a bunch of classes, audition for a Broadway show, or finish off a novel that's been stewing in my head. He makes me want to be my best self and conquer the world by his side. But is that for real? Or is he the kind of guy I would eventually wonder if I couldn't keep up with? Over the next few days, I think I'll have to balance those thoughts with my twittering heart.

DATE 14:
TYLER

I'm feeling overwhelmed. Juggling my job, and my dates, scheduling my dates, and actively assessing the changes needed in my dating habits all require more energy than I have.

I'm not getting a lot of sleep. Willingly putting myself in a constant state of vulnerability is exhausting. And the inevitable is happening—something I didn't expect but should have: I'm starting to *like* some of these guys.

It doesn't help that my friends at work are egging me on. They'll stop by my office to dish about the guys I've gone out with so far. "Jason is my favorite." "Please tell me that you love Jared as much as I do." And, "If you don't go out with Ryan again, can I?"

Sometimes we'll even rank them by desirability (and you thought men were bad!). The order will change. The reasons will change. But there is something that's becoming clear to me: Every woman's "dream guy" looks different. Where I've gone wrong in the past is that I've confused myself, imagining that I would recognize my Mr. Perfect instantly when he appeared.

Unfortunately there were times when I confused myself and my "dream" would somehow turn into "expectation." My standards (based on that picky "list" of qualities I wisely tossed aside when I began this project) would serve as a requirement for the kind of man I wanted to date. I would boast, "Oh, I *know* what I want in a man." I would quickly judge men, compare them with my imagined ideal, and disregard any serious considerations of dating them.

This way of thinking was only to my detriment. It kept me from getting the chance to meet great men who might have surprised me with their deeper potential.

The flip side of this was my insecurity when I wasn't in a relationship. On my worst days, I would allow my single status to define my self-worth. I would writhe in self-pity, "Will *any*one ever like me?" Then, once a man showed me some attention, it would break my spell of cynicism, and I would be so grateful for a date that I would do my best to fit him into my contrived parameters.

This would send me into a tailspin of neediness. One man's piqued interest could instantly trigger my switch from an empowered single gal strutting the streets of New York City to a desperate, lonely woman staring at the phone, hoping the random guy would call me. Instead of taking the time to determine whether I liked him, I would feel at his mercy. I would start to trick myself, thinking the guy was going to be my very last chance at love. *How will I meet anyone else?!* I'd think.

In many ways, I would allow my self-esteem to be defined by whether a guy found me worthy.

My reactions to men were out of balance. Either I would feel like I had full control of my dating life by rejecting or accepting a man, or I would feel powerless, as if I were lucky to have some poor sap show me any attention.

However, I'm beginning to form a better attitude about dating, which means finding that middle ground between having control and letting go. While it's good for me to have a general idea of what I want in a partner, there's much to be said for being open to other options. I need to assess guys who come my way based on who they are—not on my expectations—and accept that the next guy won't be my last chance. That attitude will make it easier for me to choose whether I want to invest my time.

I wasn't quite sure how seriously guys would take my project before it began. I wasn't sure if anyone would find it worth his time or effort. And granted, lots of guys have turned me down, saying first dates are difficult enough. Why would they want to put themselves out there for every other girl to judge them?

But then there are the guys who not only seem really interested in being part of the project, but also want to plan our date, pay for it, and do their best to impress me. I've been humbled and surprised by how kind all of the guys have been so far. Is this how men really function? Could guys really be more selfless and emotional than I've been giving them credit for my whole life? They don't really go out of their way for women like this. *Do they?*

I was set up with Tyler via my lifelong best friend, Cathy. She called me from her home outside Washington, D.C., happily reporting the latest event in her marriage: "We just got back from the emergency room!"

She was oddly elated, describing how her husband's incident with a bagel and a kitchen knife required stitches.

"Is he *okay?*"

"Oh, he's fine," she said dismissively. She clearly had more important details to discuss. "What I wanted to tell you about is the *doctor!*" He was handsome. Charming. He wasn't wearing a wedding ring. In the midst of her husband's meticulous stitching, Cathy noticed a diploma from Brigham Young University on the wall.

"He's a *Mormon,*" she said, knowing my penchant for boys of the faith. I'd already gone out with a few churchy boys. What was one more? Even if he did live four hours away. Somehow she managed to learn that no, the charming doctor wasn't seeing anyone, and yes, he did seem slightly interested in the radical dating project of her friend. They exchanged contact information, and I sent Tyler an email.

He agreed to a date, scheduled time off work from the emergency room, and made plans for a journey into the city with a girl he'd never met before.

True to the form of an emergency room doctor, he wouldn't let obstacles stand in the way of a positive outcome. He'd originally planned to catch a 3:30 AM bus from D.C., but snow on the roads slowed him down, and he arrived at the station just as the bus pulled away. Over the next three hours, he traipsed through the snow between Chinatown and Union Station, looking for a bus to New York City. He finally hopped on a Greyhound at 6:30 AM, paying twice as much for a ticket as he had originally planned. He texted me throughout the morning with updates: "Bus is running a little late!" and, "Be there by 11:30!"

I couldn't believe the sacrifice he was making. Was he that excited to see New York? The possibility of a Broadway show? Or could he actually be interested in meeting me? *It's possible, right?*

When I met Tyler outside Penn Station, he bounced toward me, greeting me with open arms. He looked like he could have arrived straight out of Provo, Utah, with a clean-cut look of nice slacks, a button-up shirt, a tight haircut, and a beaming smile, which seemed to somehow hide his tired, bloodshot eyes that nested upon dark circles.

"I made it!" he cheered.

"Welcome to New York!" I said, excited but nervous at the same time.

"Finally," he said, as if to sigh away the last eight hours.

"How was the trip?" I asked, feeling a little self-conscious and awkward about his long, determined trek to arrive here. I was having one of my "I'm not worthy" moments, but he quickly dispelled it with his good cheer and enthusiasm.

"The bus smelled like Chinese food and I tried to sleep, but I drank a bunch of caffeine and was way too stoked about getting here."

He conquered his first major feat of the day, but he still had one more big one: scoring front-row seats to see the Broadway musical *Wicked*. Every day, the theater holds a lottery to win these tickets. Tyler had tried and failed to win the prize *four* times, which I can only imagine had soured his opinion of Broadway *and* New York City.

If we won, it would cost $50 for the two front tickets. That's a *steal* for Broadway, but it's still almost twice my $31 budget. I really didn't want to break my rule, but I settled on at least paying for my own ticket. That left $6 for a couple post-show hot cocoas.

We stood among more than fifty people who swarmed around the theater door in silence, hoping the guy from the ticket booth would pull our winning names out of an orange bucket. I prayed in my head that we would win, and just then, the man with the bucket shouted Tyler's name.

Tyler jumped with joy and threw his arms around me. "We *won!*"

He bounced toward the ticket counter and slapped down $50 in cash, refusing to allow me to pay for my ticket.

"Tyler, there's no way I'm letting you pay. You just spent a bunch of money making that trip up here."

He looked at me like I was crazy. "So what? There's no *way* I'm letting you pay."

"Hey, it's a *rule!*" I blurted out, feeling a little silly and pushy. I knew he was just trying to be nice, and perhaps he even felt awkward letting me pay. Maybe he was old-school and the idea that a woman pays on the date challenged his ego. My sense was that he meant it out of generosity and a real feeling that this show had been his adventure, and he simply wanted to share the spoils. Considering all he'd done to get here, I decided to let him pay. *Anyway, aren't rules meant to be broken?* I asked myself. *Isn't this what the project is all about?*

He looked at me, pleading, and I relented.

"Oh, all right. But I owe you hot cocoa!"

Tyler's caffeine-induced energy seemed to spike over the next hour or so before the show began. He would scurry around happily with the zest of a Jack Russell terrier. He kept tugging my arm in bursts of excitement. "I can't believe we won tickets to see *Wicked!*"

The doors to the theater opened, and we walked with pride to the front row. The gentleman sitting next to us beamed, "Well, *hello, winners!*" We peered down into the orchestra pit right in front of us and watched the musicians warm up. As the curtain rose, Tyler grabbed my arm again. "It's starting!" He leaned to me during the show with bits of commentary. "I can't believe we're here!" and "That woman is *so perfect* in her role!" or "Do you ever wonder which of the guys is straight and which is gay?"

Yes. I do.

He loved the storyline, which is the backstory of *The Wizard of Oz* and explains why the Wicked Witch of the West might not be so wicked after all, but maybe just misunderstood.

"I just think it's amazing how a story can *completely change* when you look at it from someone else's angle."

Yes. It is, I thought. I was learning that in spades.

After the show ended, we walked in the rain by Times Square, headed toward Grand Central Station, and made our way back by Bryant Park. He exuded pure delight the whole day, looking wide-eyed at the buildings as if it were his first time seeing skyscrapers. He soaked in every detail of the city.

We grabbed those hot chocolates I promised, and Tyler started asking all sorts of random questions, wondering about my favorite books and movies and seeing what else I liked to do for fun. I couldn't tell if he was really interested, making small talk, or trying to see if I was fulfilling some list he'd made for his dream girl.

"Favorite comedy?" he asked.

"I like chick flicks and slapstick," I said, feeling my answers were definitely not on his list.

He laughed. "Well, that's okay. Chick flicks are good every now and then, right?"

I couldn't really figure Tyler out. Was he always this upbeat or was he just trying to compensate for being overly tired? I couldn't keep up. After going nonstop on dates for two weeks with just a few hours of sleep a night, I was haggard and there was no way I could hide it. And yet, there was Tyler, laughing sleeplessness off and celebrating his adventure. I longed for his enthusiasm—to a degree. If his intense attitude were natural and constant, there was no way I could endure a guy like that. I need downtime.

The more we talked, the more I learned that he was indeed always *on*. In addition to his round-the-clock work in the emergency room, he travels the world helping the needy, chats with teens about drug dangers, and regularly whisks away for fun adventures. *Is he now trying to give me answers he thinks are on MY list?*

I couldn't imagine how one man could do so much with his time, constantly running around trying to save the world. How would he ever have time to really date? Where would a woman fit into his schedule? Really, Tyler was living life to the fullest, and here I was judging his efforts, feeling jealous of his endurance and feeling as if it would be impossible for me to measure up. And I wasn't quite sure if I wanted to. I didn't want to feel as if I'd passed some test, meeting the qualifications on some guy's list. I just wanted things to feel natural.

And then I remembered my own lists that I'd made. How much had I held on to my shallow ideals in the past? How much did my own desires for some "dream guy" stand in the way of genuinely getting to know someone and respecting him for his unique self? I tried to get our conversation past the superficial level and get real. I wanted to really understand Tyler. Was he really as intense as he seemed?

"So Tyler," I asked, "was seeing a Broadway show the only reason for crawling your way through a blizzard? Or did you find something about me or my silly dating project intriguing?" I'm usually not so forward, but I figured this type of approach was needed. I had to figure him out.

He seemed to soften a little. I might have even seen him take a second to breathe, relaxing into a state of comfort and familiarity with me. "Well," he said, "I did actually debate for a while whether to take the day off work and make the trip, but eventually I just decided to do it."

"But why? Because you wanted to see *Wicked?* Am I the beard here?" I teased.

He paused for a second and shrugged. "I thought you seemed like fun and thought, *Why not?*"

"That's quite the risk, isn't it?" I asked, a little startled by how challenging I sounded.

"Is it?" he asked, smiling.

Good question . . .

He seemed less intense, more kind. Like any good doctor—the type of guy I'd want by my side in crisis.

We made our way back to Penn Station so he could began his journey back to Washington. "So," he asked, "any chance you'll be visiting Cathy in D.C. soon? Maybe we could have a double date? It'd be good to see those guys outside the emergency room."

I nodded. "I'll let you know next time I head down," I said, unsure if we would actually have that second date. Had I measured up? Had he? I was too tired to tell. As I sunk into my couch after getting home, I started to feel an amalgam of emotions flood over me.

I started to cry. And it wasn't one of those soft, whimpering cries. It was a full-body, breath-gasping, lip-quivering wail. I felt overwhelmingly humbled and undeserving. My old insecure feelings of being unworthy and generally unlovable seemed to rise to the surface.

Am I taking advantage of all these nice guys for my own selfish purposes? Is this project really doing anyone any good? Am I just wasting my time? Are the guys?

In the back of my mind, reason fluttered. I knew I was overtired, overstimulated, and overextended. Anything could set me off. I figured I needed reinforcement from someone who really understood me.

So I called my mom, and I let it all out.

"I can't do it anymore," I cried wildly. "It's *so much* more work than I thought it would be. I have to plan *everything*, spend *so* much time meeting people, and then who *knows* if I'm even someone worth being around. This was the *dumbest idea* I've ever had. *Why* am I even doing this?" I wailed.

"You sound tired," she said.

"I'm exhausted!" I moaned. "I'm getting no sleep! I keep dragging myself around the city. And why? *Why* am I doing this? Can I just quit? *No one* thinks this project is a good idea anyway!"

I could tell that my mother, who is kind and reasonable, was staying calm and collected for me on purpose. "No one thinks this is a good idea? Who has told you that?"

"Mom," I argued through my tears and stuffy nose, "It *is* stupid. No one has to say it. It just *is.*"

"Well," she said pointedly, "*I* don't think it's stupid. Your *friends* don't think it's stupid. Or do we not count because we *love you?* You've had tons of strangers tell you they're excited for you. Even *Diane Sawyer* thinks it's a good idea. So what else do you *need?* Who else do you need to tell you this is not stupid?"

Her reason had silenced my crying a bit. "I don't know . . . "

"Who?" she insisted. "*Who* do you need to tell you this is a good idea for you to feel good about it?"

"I guess," I said, realizing my words as I said them aloud, "I guess I need *myself* to think it's a good idea."

"Good," she said, with a mother's proud tone. "Look. No one is forcing you to do this. If you need to quit now, it'll be okay. People will understand."

"Mom," I said, sounding like a sassy teenager, "I'm *not* gonna quit. I'm just *tired.*"

"Good," she said. "Now go to bed."

I discovered upon waking that sleep is good medicine. And I didn't even need my friendly doctor to tell me that.

DATE 15: GABRIEL

A few years ago I decided to run a marathon. Most runners will "hit the wall" during a long race, usually toward the end. Me? I hit the wall halfway through. At mile thirteen I could feel my self-doubt creeping in. I felt exhausted, dehydrated, and unprepared, even though I spent months training. *Who am I kidding?* I thought. *I'm not a REAL runner. I'm not cut out for a marathon.* My head-trip slowed me down. I was exponentially physically and emotionally drained. My calves tightened as I dragged one foot in front of the other. My eyes glazed over as I watched old ladies speed-walk past me. I wanted to cry, but I couldn't waste the last drop of water in my body on tears. Despite the shortness of my breath, the blisters ripping against my socks, my swollen hands, and the insanely tired voice whining words of self-doubt in my head, I was too determined to quit. Eventually, something kicked in. Whatever it was, I picked up my pace, kept moving, ignored the blisters, the fear, the doubt, and finally finished.

I guess it makes sense that I would also hit the wall during what feels like the endurance sport of dating.

My friends—work and otherwise—continue offering their support. Amy is keeping things in perspective through fractions: "You're halfway there! It's normal to feel a slump at the halfway point. But in just a few days, you'll be two-thirds done!" And Lumina's poetic advice is helping me feel a little better today. "Being excellent is difficult," she says. "You're at the hard part. The part where ordinary people give up. You have to keep working hard for a little while longer. Just like the marathon, babe. You got this. One step after one step."

Her advice made tonight's date with Gabriel seem even more providential. We would be taking huge steps together by climbing an indoor rock wall.

What better way to get over hitting the wall, eh? And I'd be too busy seeking out handholds to mull over last night's meltdown and my fragile sense of purpose.

Gabe doesn't look like the rock-climbing type to me. He's tall, lanky, and clean cut. He's a computer software engineer who doesn't say much but smiles and nods in amusement when I talk too much about my busy day at work.

He admits to being more of an introvert who tends to have fun at home playing computer games, watching movies, or hanging out with friends. I generally get along well with men like this; maybe it's because they remind me of my brother, Darren. Gabe, in particular, is like him—the type of guy who has fun but never finds himself in the center of the crowd. Instead, like Gabe, he enjoys spending time figuring out computers. In fact, when a friend of a friend suggested

Gabe consider being part of my project, he scoped my website to see what kind of techie techniques I used. "So, do you know HTML?" he asked.

"The basics," I exaggerated. "I've been learning as I go." *Since when have I been able to understand computer lingo?*

"I noticed you're using Analytics to measure your number of blog readers. How many people are reading your site?"

"How did you notice I was using that program? People can see that kind of stuff?"

He smiled with pride. "Only if you know where to look."

Gabe wasn't going to let me get away with thinking of him as just a geeky hacker. He quickly revealed that underneath his shy exterior, he craves outdoor adventure—but not just anything. He's a thrill-seeker.

"These days I spend a lot of time riding my motorcycle," he explained.

"*You* ride a *motorcycle?*" I couldn't hide my surprise at the conflicting idea of "weekday computer geek" somehow strapping on leather bike chaps and a bandanna to become "weekend boss of the hog."

Wow. A complex man. Who'da thunk?

I was suddenly a little more intrigued by quiet guy with a pocket protector.

He laughed, as if he'd expected—and maybe even hoped—that I would be shocked. Oh, and he sails . . . *and* has all his own rock-climbing equipment.

Before meeting up with Gabe, I wasn't really sure whether he was my type, so I wasn't feeling the same level of first-date jitters I might feel with someone I expected I might be more attracted to. Nonetheless, I felt ill at ease. You see, not only am I afraid of heights, but I'm also afraid of making a total ass out of myself.

And I managed to look like an idiot for much of the date.

Case in point: As I rushed to the rock-climbing studio, I flung open the door and banged my head on its side. A few minutes later, I sat waiting for Gabe, holding an ice pack to the huge welt rising on my eyebrow. When he arrived, I was obviously flustered. We walked up the stairs and I slipped, dropping my purse, my camera, and my wallet. I was a klutz, and I hadn't even begun climbing yet.

Maybe it's a good thing that he doesn't say much, after all.

I changed clothes in the locker room, sat down on a bench, and took in a deep breath, hoping to relax a little. I felt drained and unsure about whether I had the stamina—physical, spiritual, emotional—to complete the entire dating project.

Fifteen more to go—no, fifteen and a half. Sigh . . . Come on, girl, you can do it.

I looked in the mirror and looked at the outfit I had just changed into: a sports bra, yoga pants, an old T-shirt.

Great. Am I really hitting the halfway mark wearing my pajamas?

The climbing room looked (and unfortunately smelled) like a small, dark high school gym packed with people and the stench of old sweat. The climbers looked like they were from the same team, with their similar outdoorsy look: thin, strong, and long, with unkempt hair. Guys were skipping up the wall with the ease of Spider Man. For a second, I secretly wished the gym would close before I got my chance to climb.

Gabe showed me how to put on the climbing gear, and we made our way into the mass of hard-core climbers. An instructor explained the tricks and terms, showing me how to put on my harness (a series of straps that ridiculously emphasizes my bulging butt) and how to belay properly (a safety feature to make sure I don't fall to my death), and he informed me that I was going to be in charge of Gabe's rope as he climbed (almost a 100 percent chance that I would mess up and drop him). Was he kidding me? I had just met Gabe and already he was putting his life into my hands.

While I stand a meek five-three, Gabriel is about six and a half feet tall. For extra precautions and more weight to balance out our twelve-inch-plus height difference, I needed to be *secured to the ground*. Seriously. I was locked to the ground, with my butt-enhanced harness strapped to nylon ropes and carabiners. I had no idea what I was doing, and my heart was beating so hard I could feel it pulsate in my stomach.

Gabe yelled the proper command to me as he prepared to begin his journey. "On belay?"

I looked to my instructor for guidance and recalled the phrase that meant I was ready for him to begin. "Belay on!"

He grabbed on to the wall and made his first climb. Somehow I kept his rope secure and actually made sure he didn't fall too quickly. Whenever I showed fear, he would reassure me, "You're doing great!"

Then it was my turn. And I immediately questioned the wisdom of putting myself in a stranger's hands—literally—on our first date. When Gabe first suggested it over email, I responded with a loud "YES!" But now that I was actually walking toward the wall with all my bulky gear, my insecurities surfaced. I was sure everyone would watch and judge me. Not to mention, I was about to climb up and possibly freak out and fall, and my rear end would be sticking out for everyone to see. But it was too late. I had made it this far. I could make it to the top.

My big challenge stood before me in the form of a giant wall with fake rocks nailed to it. Gabe was a gentle cheerleader. "You're an adrenaline junkie, right?" he asked. "Climbing is perfect for you."

Is that true?

I headed to the wall and found my first step. I reached up and over for my first hold on the wall. Once I got five feet above ground, it felt a little easier. I no longer felt intimidated by the vertical barrier. The climb became fun, almost like a puzzle I was trying to solve. And soon enough, I had made my way to the top and had no fear as I looked down at Gabe, holding a firm grip on my rope. Gabe slowly repelled me, and I floated down to the ground. I jumped up and down like a little kid and applauded for myself. A couple of the hard-core climbers clapped along with me.

"See?" said Gabe. "You're a climber now."

The entire pajama-wearing, butt-flying, climbing experience seemed intimidating—even scary—initially, but once I found my groove (quite literally), my confidence grew. Of course, I couldn't help but translate this to dating. How much did I really put myself out there, really take chances and extend myself way beyond my comfort zone? Every day, I and millions of other men and women are putting ourselves out there, despite the sheer terror of meeting someone new, the possibility of looking stupid, and the lack of knowing what will happen. *Will I fall? Will I land on my feet?* But the reward is worth it: reaching the top. Maybe even finding true love.

DATE 16: BRIAN

Years ago I was in a pretty serious relationship with a tall, skinny DJ who spun records at raves and big parties. People were drawn to his quick wit and chill attitude. He had lots of friends, smoked lots of pot, and made little money. The two years we spent together must have worn both of us down. We started to act like siblings snipping back at one another. Our spats would crescendo and my volume would peak in frustration. "WELL, what do you WANT FROM ME?!"

He would raise his lanky arms as if pleading to the gods for help. "I just want to make you happy!" he screamed. "Just TELL ME what I need to do to make you HAPPY!"

It wasn't until this week that I finally understood what my DJ actually meant. It was simple: He really did want me to be happy. And I'm starting to believe that most men want this, too, because the men I've gone out with so far for this dating project really seem to find joy from seeing me smile.

Sure, I realize that most of these guys are putting on their best behavior for my project. After all, they know I intend to write about them. But I'm starting to understand that I play a bigger role in whether men treat me well than I've been giving myself credit for. It's as if the more I allow men to treat me well, the more they go out of their way to do so, and the more happy and confident they appear to be. It's a nice cycle of my being genuinely thankful and their happily showing me kindness.

Honestly, the act of "receiving" is not very natural or easy for me. The tough career-girl feminist inside me screams, *I can open my own doors, thank you very much. I can handle it.*

I became so accustomed to working hard, making lists, checking them off, and succeeding, that I didn't take the time to let go and relax. I had been pushing so hard for love that I wasn't able to step back and receive. Just like sowing and reaping, I needed to realize that in the midst of all of my hard work, I needed to also sit back and enjoy the fruits of my labor.

Thinking of myself as a "receiver" has my head spinning a bit. I've been thinking a lot about the jerks and the players I've dealt with—all those guys who were cruel, who tried just to get in my pants and move on. How would I have reacted to them differently in the past had I walked around with a receiving mindset like *I will allow you to treat me well* or *I will be open to the love you have to offer?* Would I have been able to separate the good guys from the dirtbags a little better?

This perspective of "good men want to make women happy" has me feeling a little more in love with men in general. My crush level has spiked. I feel a little more bouncy and upbeat.

I was high on my "I love men" kick when I met Brian. And then he threw me for a loop.

At forty years old, Brian is the oldest person I've ever gone out with. He typically dates women he meets online, which made sense when I learned he found out about me through my website. He suggested that we meet early, at the New York Transit Museum in Brooklyn, which is basically the Smithsonian of the New York subway system, only a million times smaller. And underground.

When I arrived at 9:00 AM, Brian was waiting outside, looking debonair in a suit and tie. He had planned our day down to a science and emailed me a brief outline of our schedule. I wasn't quite sure I could keep up with this dapper dating pro.

We walked down the stairs into an old subway station redesigned into one of the coolest museums I've ever seen. Brian slapped down $12 for our entry fee.

"I know you've offered to pay for these dates, but there's absolutely no way I'm letting you pay for me."

I'd heard this gripe from some of the guys before. I wasn't offended by his insistence on paying as some way of proving his masculinity or anything. I think he's just old school. "Traditional." Which is fine, but I was beginning to think he was going a little overboard with the chivalry. His overly outlined date, paired with his insistence on paying, felt a bit superficial. Like maybe I was with a tour guide, rather than on a real date.

As we maneuvered through the old turnstiles, original subway train cars, and refurbished clunky metal machines, I felt strangely like I was in another era, maybe even another league, dating a man this age. He seemed to take the idea of a "date" way more seriously than other guys, much like I imagine my parents—maybe even my grandparents—did. I debated his intentions. Was he just trying to match my own extensive efforts that I'd made when outlining my project? Was he showing off? I couldn't figure it out. Maybe it was just taking us both a while to warm up to each other.

I decided to keep my focus on the museum, which somehow made me feel even younger than I was already feeling. It was like I was a little kid with a wide grin, skipping through train cars from the 1920s, '50s, and '70s. I imagined what it must have been like to be a passenger on board, cruising through the decades of changing sites in New York.

After an hour touring the museum, Brian announced the next part of his plan. "We're pretty much on schedule so far," he said. "You ready to check out more of Brooklyn?" He escorted me outside, where we spotted a food truck.

"I noticed from reading about your other dates online that you seem to really like hot chocolate. Would you like some?" he asked.

I blushed at his interest. *He'd even read what I've written about my other dates?* Maybe I'd judged him too quickly. Too harshly. Maybe he was just a guy who'd spent time learning about me and my project and was now just trying to show his best side. After all, he had mentioned he was into theater. Maybe this was just his way of putting on a show. Or maybe he really was just doing his best to be chivalrous and I needed to get over it.

Remember how you're trying to practice "receiving," missy? I smiled, a little embarrassed. "Brian, I would love a hot chocolate."

As we walked by historical sites, Brian narrated our journey with factual tidbits.

"That big building is Borough Hall," he said, pointing to what looked like a smaller and less extravagant version of the U.S. Capitol. "It was actually the first city hall in Brooklyn."

Clearly, he knew quite a bit about the exhibits. I did my best to play the part of happy-girl-on-a-tour as we passed the Brooklyn Public Library, which had a surprisingly wide, barren facade and looked like it could easily be mistaken for a top-secret government location.

"It looks so uninviting," I said.

"Maybe you just need to look at it a little differently," he said as he took a few steps back to get a good look at the entire building. "If you look at the whole thing, it looks like an open book. See how the entryway looks like a spine? And then the two long wings off to the side are the cover and back cover." He looked at his watch with self-assurance. "Looks like we're right on schedule."

"Brian, you are by far the most precise planner I've ever met," I said, smiling and shaking my head. I was beginning to find his methodical dating strategy endearing, quirky, and totally amusing.

He smiled back. "Well, do you know why I gave you so much information ahead of time?" he asked.

"I figured you were being nice."

He shook his head as if I had failed a pop quiz, which annoyed me a little. As if I were an ignorant student and not his equal.

"No, no, no," he said. "I wanted you to know the plans. You know. In case you needed to tell other people where you were going with some guy you'd never met. For safety."

Safety?

All of a sudden I realized the many situations in the last few hours in which Brian could have harmed me: strangling me and stashing my body in a 1950s subway car or bonking my head with a book and dumping my body in the book-return chute at the Brooklyn Public Library.

Okay, great. Now I felt stupid. I thought requiring my dates to be held in "public places" was enough of a safety precaution. But was it? After all, I'd been merrily prancing around the city with random guys at all hours and letting tango dancers try to feel me up on the dance floor. Where was Brian's dating guidance before I got started with this whole project?

"How do you know all this stuff?" I asked.

"I'm single and forty," he said, shrugging his shoulders with a smile. "I date a lot."

It was as if I were an apprentice learning dating tricks and tips from the master.

"Also," he said earnestly, "you could always use your bail-out phone call."

"Hmm," I registered. I'd heard of girls making those "safe calls" before, but I always thought that idea was a little more cautious—or even neurotic—than I wanted to be. But what do I know? Maybe I'd been naive all these years. Brian's analysis was starting to make me question every move I'd ever made on dates.

"I swear. It happens all the time with women I meet online. They'll get a phone call about thirty minutes into the date.

Then say something like, 'Oh, Mom, that's so great! Can I call you later?' And I'll ask, 'Is that your getaway phone call in case I'm crazy and you need to leave?' They always seem surprised that I know what's going on. I think it's smart. I can respect that."

Nice. Brian surprised me. On the one hand, I felt he was a bit patronizing, but on the other hand, he clearly respected the single-gal protocol. Not just respected, but supported it.

We continued our tour, stopping by a marble statue in the Brooklyn Museum, and he looked at the figures with awe. Is was a classic Rodin sculpture, and he talked about it as if he were in love.

"This is one of my most favorites," he mentioned dreamily. "Do you see the intricate details of each of the men in this piece? It took Rodin twenty years to do this. Can you imagine investing twenty years in anything?"

I mean, could I? Twenty *years?* With anything? *Anyone?* I have a hard enough time committing to my cell phone provider for two years. Could I actually love something—or someone— enough to want to be with him *forever?* Here I was, easily bouncing from a bunch of "practice dates" with myriad men. How hard would it be, actually investing my heart, time, and energy in just one guy? Did I have that emotional endurance anymore?

As Brian and I walked, he opened up more, and we fell into a pattern of conversation where I felt more his equal and less a pupil to his "wiser, older man" persona. For several years he's dreamed of working for the State Department and has spent months preparing and studying for the tough entry exam. I liked his dedication and relentless pursuit of what he loves, like running every day around Prospect Park, or remaining an avid cyclist, even though he's been hit by a car *seven times*. He doesn't let the tough times get him down.

A girl could take a cue from that perseverance.

Especially when it comes to dating. Sure, I might have embarked on a whirlwind thirty-one-date experience, but for Brian it's a lifestyle—he goes out on at least one date every week, mostly with women he meets online. All in the pursuit of grander love. As he talked about the shift in women's attitudes as he's gotten older—about how they relate to him differently now that he's forty—I felt an affinity with him in terms of the struggle to find an authentic relationship as we grow older.

"Women don't seem to mind dating a guy in his thirties," he explained. "But when I turned forty, it seemed like women started wondering what's wrong with me. Like, why haven't I settled down?"

Admittedly, I'm one of those women, wondering the same thing. What's keeping this guy single so long? Considering how much effort he put into planning our date, I can only imagine he's someone who fully commits to everything he does. It seems like he's the type of guy who'd do everything for the woman he loves. Plus, he's smart, kind, and totally energetic. He might have a traditional approach to dating, but he's far from a fuddy-duddy. Maybe Brian just hasn't found the right person.

I so relate.

"So, how's your project coming along?" he asked. "Have you met some interesting guys?"

"I have," I admitted, and I was suddenly flooded with a surge of near giddiness as I reflected on my growing fondness for some of the men I'd met. *These feelings could be real! I might have found some men I actually want to be with! Who seem to like me, too! Miracles are happening! The world is wonderful, and beautiful, and blessing me with love!*

"Oh, that's good," he quipped. "Because it's not like this project lends itself to actually finding anyone to date seriously."

His casual cynicism knocked me for a loop, and my rose-tinted glass fogged instantly. Was he right?

After all, when I first began this project, I just assumed there was no chance I could ever actually meet anyone through something so contrived. This was nothing but a project. A social experiment. A game. A structured class to teach me about how I'm a disaster in love and all things dating related. Brian must be right, I thought. Considering all his own dating experience . . . Of course! What does one manufactured night together foster between two people, anyway? Where was my head?!

"Yeah," I nodded, acting as if his look of prideful endorsement wasn't actually veiled condescension. "You're right. This is totally not the way to meet anyone."

"But," he said, smiling in genuine support, "it seems like a really fun experiment."

At that moment, I was sure he was going to pat me on the back like he might his sister or, worse, his daughter.

I had started the day thinking men wanted women to be happy, and all I needed to do was lovingly "receive" the goodness they had to offer. Should I be "receiving" Brian's suggestion? Was I fooling myself into thinking any of these guys could really like me? And when did this project become about finding love and not learning?

I needed to get my head straight—that was certain. Especially since I was only just now turning the corner on the second half of the project.

DATE 17: PETER

I danced and skipped happily around Central Park, feeling the cold air spin across my face as I twirled. The *clang* of church bells chimed four times from a huge clock standing high on a three-tiered brick tower. At the base of the clock, fanciful statues spun around like a carousel: A bronze bear waved a tambourine, a hippopotamus stroked a violin, and a penguin banged a drum. They revolved around the clock as a familiar song rang through the air. I sang along loudly.

> *"Row, row, row your boat,*
> *Gently down the stream.*
> *Merrily, merrily, merrily, merrily,*
> *Life is but a dream!"*

Merrily, Peter and I roamed the park, our playground for the day. We ran to the top of Belvedere Castle and breathlessly declared victory over our kingdom. We spied on a puppet show at the small Swedish Cottage and then climbed rocks on our way to the Central Park Zoo.

With Peter, I felt as if I had been given full permission to act like a five-year-old. This was a good challenge for me, since I don't easily act silly and childish with people I've just met. Especially coming off a date with a more buttoned-down man—more sophisticated, less whimsical. One who had grounded me firmly in reality. Peter was the perfect counterpoint. Today, I just wanted to be free and enjoy myself. Constantly being around new people and allowing myself to let my guard down is sometimes challenging, but I've started feeling the shift in my anxiety about whether I'm presenting my most perfect self on each date. For me, I feel like this is the beginning of a breakthrough—and that makes sense to me, considering the sharp peaks and valleys of this experience so far. I'm *learning*.

Dating a bunch of different guys brings out different parts of my personality. It shakes things up a bit. They each ask different questions and enjoy different aspects of life. Having so many dates so close together also helps me realize easily which types of men naturally bring out the full spectrum of my personality. Their differences have helped me gain a deeper appreciation for mankind. And kind men.

Peter found me through my blog and thought my project sounded fun. He drove an hour to the city from his home in Rockland County, New York. He's younger than I am and looks it, with his cute, boyish face and big dimples. He's just a little taller than I am, dresses casually in jeans and a shirt, and has both ears pierced, wearing round, silver studs, which looked unexpected worn alongside his conservative haircut.

It was my idea to hit the Central Park Zoo. He hadn't seen much of Central Park, and the zoo seemed like just the right place to get a good dose of the landscape while giving us a place to play all day. We split the entry fee, which cost each of us $12. So far, I'd done really well keeping the $31-or-less rule, but most of the guys wouldn't let me pay the whole way. Just another lesson learned, and I was fine with it. At least they were honoring my price limit, which required a lot of creativity and time spent searching for frugal dates.

For those who haven't been to the zoo here, it's the epito-me of New York housing, squeezing lots of animals into a small lot. It's home to flamingos, penguins, and even polar bears. It also has bats, which Peter shuddered at, and snakes, which made *me* squirm.

By far, the biggest attraction is a gigantic pool of sea lions. Peter and I were like children, running along the side of the pool, chasing the sea lions as they swam. We may have even knocked over a few children in the bargain—we were that relentless. Just as we'd find a pace to match theirs, they would dart off to the other side of the tank and pop their whiskered noses up above water, where children (the ones still standing) squealed with joy.

"Hey, how come they aren't coming to see us?" I mock-whined.

"Well, I guess at least you know something about me now," he said jokingly. "I'm not good with sea lions."

Suddenly, the expression on Peter's face changed. He looked, well, gleeful and mischievous. He walked away from the tank, toward a door that read NO ADMITTANCE, and did his best to open it and look inside.

"Peter!" I shouted, "What are you doing?" I felt a sudden concern about needing to follow the rules.

He laughed at my worry. "There's nothing back there anyway."

We had fulfilled our childlike roles: He was the boy who caused a ruckus. I was the goody-two-shoes who would end up as the tattletale.

"I like doing things that are inappropriate," he said.

"Inappropriate? Like what?"

"Not, like, *illegal,* but I definitely like doing things that go against social standards." I laughed and rolled my eyes. He was definitely a little mischievous. And I was his overly responsible counterpart. Maybe the change in outlook would do me some good.

We walked a few yards to the children's petting zoo to see little goats, llamas, and lambs that were squeaking to their moms. I've never really been a huge fan of zoos. Like Peter said, they're kind of sad. I realize that the animals are treated really well, but there's something about so many animals in cages that makes me feel a little sorry for them. Which makes me want to be extra friendly to the little guys.

I grabbed some alfalfa from a bubble-gum machine by cranking the silver handle a couple times and cupping my hands beneath the chute. A black goat must have heard the familiar sound, because he walked toward me with determination. *You're mine,* he seemed to say. I reached out my hand to feed him. He tipped his nose upward and his thick, rough tongue swept against my hand, lapping the pebbles of food. "Ewwwwwww!" I giggled with happy disgust. I petted the top of his head, surprised that his fur felt coarse and not soft, as I expected.

"You are my most favorite goat ever," I said, and moved on. I was so happy to feel so free and silly on a date. Peter just seemed to bring out my carefree side, which I loved, even if that meant getting slobbered on by a goat.

In the next pen, Peter spotted a cow. "You think they'll care if I go in with him?"

"Does it matter?" I quipped. It was easy—and kind of fun—to play the "straight man" to his goofball. I could enjoy his antics without putting myself on the line. *Hmmm. I'm seeing a parallel!*

He looked around to see if anyone was watching, then put one leg through the fence, weaving his way through to the other side. The cow strolled to Peter as if they were old friends. Peter's eyes beamed.

"Peter, you're the youngest child in your family, aren't you?" I asked, already knowing the answer.

He turned to look at me as if I'd solved some sort of riddle. "How'd you know?"

"Are you *kidding?* You try to get away with *everything.*"

We both laughed, but his devilish grin faded as his hand held still on the cow's head. "Let me put it this way—I have a *lot* of brothers and sisters."

"Oh, nice," I said, flip. "I bet *that* was fun growing up."

By the look on his face, I clearly wasn't getting what he meant.

"No, I mean *a lot* of siblings," he said. "I have *thirteen* brothers and sisters."

The numbers took a few seconds to gel. "You mean, you're the youngest of *fourteen kids?*" I imagined what his home must have been like growing up, with older siblings toting toddlers on their hips as they helped in the kitchen. At night, the children might have taken several rotating shifts in the bathroom before piling into bedrooms at night.

I assumed he came from a devout family—maybe Catholic (considering their rules about contraception)—and given his name, I could only imagine he was preceded by Matthew, Mark, Luke, James, John, Mary, Joseph, et cetera. His mischievous spirit started to make sense. I imagined his family was close-knit, warm-hearted, and law-abiding. And then there was Peter, the self-proclaimed black sheep, befriending a cow.

In some ways, I could relate with trying to go against the ways you've known for so long. I understood what it felt like to be somewhat of a caged animal hungering for escape.

When it came to relationships, I was trapped by my own bad habits. Peter was crossing boundary lines—and enjoying himself—without causing anyone any harm. I could stand to learn a lesson. Today was a good move. I definitely slipped through the bars a little by letting myself have fun, be goofy, and be totally unconcerned about whether I looked, sounded, or acted cool. Who knows, after today, I might just check the next NO ADMITTANCE door I see. But . . . I think I'll stop shy of getting in the cowpen with Peter.

DATE 18: JONATHAN

It was the first day of February, and there wasn't a cloud in the sky. As I looked at the ocean's horizon, I felt a cool breeze whip up from the tide. The weather was mild, and I was in the company of a man who seemed to exist only in my dreams: tall, blond, blue-eyed, charming smile.

It was my Heaven.

Jonathan came highly recommended from my friend Megan, who described him as witty and handsome. She forgot to mention that his yumminess would startle me into a swoon.

In my email exchanges with Jonathan, I asked him to give me a basic description of himself so I would know who to look for when we met.

"Here's a picture of what I look like," he wrote. "See you soon," and attached a photo of himself. My eyes grew big and my jaw dropped. *There's NO WAY this is actually a picture of him. He's too good looking. This has got to be a model or something.*

I kept clicking back to his email and gaping at his photo. *How am I going to keep myself from staring at his pretty face the whole time we're together? Wait, forget that. How am I going to keep myself from* kissing *that pretty face?* Guys who looked that hot didn't really exist in my world. He was movie star hot. I mean, he put Brad Pitt to shame. The problem? I had already decided I wasn't good enough for him.

Jonathan suggested we meet on Coney Island—usually known as a summer beach spot—claiming it was also great to visit in winter. I trusted his judgment, since he's spent most of his life in New York, although his family and work have taken him all over the world.

I couldn't hear enough about his life. I was smitten almost on contact. And it didn't help that he had a very soft hint of a British accent from living in England as a child. He spoke words like "boardwalk" and "water" a little more gently than the typical American, perhaps with a little less "r." Whatever the case, I had to resist asking him to say those words over again. Maybe there was even a little Canadian in there as well? After all, he holds citizenship there, too. *I wonder if he speaks French . . .*

I kept my shoes on as we walked on the crunchy sand. He told me how his changing career has taken him all over the world.

"I actually started out working in your industry," he said, "as a journalist."

I stopped walking long enough to digest his stories about the news business. Discovering his passion for reporting made my heart pitter-patter with delight. I felt a romantic cliché pop into my head as I reached—okay, maybe even stretched—for our cosmic connection: *We have so much in common!*

In a nutshell, Jonathan studied journalism in college and then worked as a newspaper reporter in different cities—including Paris. *Yep. He must speak French. Mon Dieu!* After Paris, he became a . . . hero. That's right. He enlisted in the Marines and was sent to fight in the war in Iraq.

Is it possible for me to fall in love with him this quickly?

Obviously, no. But I was crushing big-time.

After four years of military service, he came back to the city, where he found a job in what's typically known as the dark side of journalism—public relations. Dark side? No biggie if it's someone like Jonathan. Heck, it didn't matter to me if he became Darth Vader himself; I was falling *hard*.

Okay, so you're probably saying, "Tamara, we get it. He's gorgeous, wordly, heroic, *and* he's a writer. But what about substance? What's beyond that smoking visage?"

You mean that's not enough? Well, not only is he tall and handsome, but he has a sweet, dry sense of humor (which will slay me every time). His voice—did I mention his voice?—has a gentle, rich timbre, and he speaks with a humble intelligence, as if his world travels, his hard work, and his military service were no big deal. "Going into the Marines just made sense to me," he said, shrugging his shoulders. "It's just war. What's the worst that could happen, right?" he said, smiling.

"Well, you're way braver than I am," I said.

He didn't respond, but his eyes belied what must have been a soul-wrenching experience. His flip response clearly veiled deeper convictions. He changed the subject.

"How about we go grab a slice?" he suggested. "I know a great pizza place just a couple blocks from here. It's supposed to be one of the top five in New York."

I was floored by how much life he'd lived, how much wisdom and maturity he seemed to possess—at least compared with me. *Yep,* I thought disheartedly. *He's definitely out of my league.*

I kicked the sand off my feet as we stepped up onto the boardwalk. A group of older women in fur coats chatted in Russian, looking like they were enjoying a Sunday stroll. We passed several older couples who huddled together on benches, holding hands and silently staring at the ocean.

The romance was killing me. I would have held his hand in a heartbeat.

We walked by a long fence that enclosed what was once Coney Island's amusement park. I noticed a dog pawing and biting at the fence, trying to get out. I rushed to see if he was okay and saw that he was bleeding. "Oh no!" I gasped, and walked closer and noticed the big gash on his mouth. My starry-eyed focus on Jonathan dissipated quickly as I crouched down and sulked at his sweet, sad face chewing on the fence. All the lessons I'd had in dog training had failed with Watson, but I thought the commands I knew would work on that poor, bleeding pup.

I looked behind me, hoping Jonathan wouldn't hear me. I felt a tiny bit of shame worrying about what he'd think if he heard me, but my better sense kicked in. "Leave it!" I commanded.

The dog released his tightened jaw from the fence, lay down, and looked at me with a whimper. I whimpered back.

I heard Jonathan's voice behind me. "Hey," he said, "let me go grab those cops over there." He jogged over to a police car sitting on the side of the boardwalk.

"Hey!" he called to them. "There's a dog in there bleeding!" He pointed to the fence.

The officers looked at me and the dog, both of us wearing pitiful expressions. "We'll take care of it, miss," they said, "don't worry."

As they drove off, I felt embarrassed about how much emotion I had just shown. I wasn't ready to show that much vulnerability around Jonathan.

"Sorry," I said, "I kind of have a soft spot for animals."

"Me too," he said.

Is that true? Or is he just trying to make me feel less awkward?

"Well," he explained, "I mean, I like dogs at least."

When we finally made our way to the pizza place, I ordered a plate-size slice of hot, gooey cheese pizza, folded the piece lengthwise, and attempted to take small, dainty bites without getting grease everywhere while trying to pay attention to every word Jonathan said. I listened intently, as if needing to mentally download every detail about his favorite sports teams, his roommates, his photography class, while insecure thoughts drifted through my head. *How weird do I look chewing this pizza? Am I spilling sauce on myself? Getting pepper in my teeth?*

I swallowed a bite and wiped my mouth as I muffled, "Why in the world would you want to be part of a project like mine?"

"Why not?"

The perfect answer for what was already a perfect day. Mr. Wonderful made me nervous, even when we said goodbye.

He wrapped his arms around me confidently, and I wondered how he looked at me. As a friend? A potential girlfriend? A little sister who loved puppies?

"You take care," he said. "Hopefully we get to see each other again sometime."

"I'd love that," I said, looking into his eyes one last time, feeling about as vulnerable as that stray dog. Did I see reflected back the possibility of a future? Or was I simply seeing my own desires reflected back?

Only time would tell.

DATE 19: KEVIN

Consecutively going out on first dates is helping me better understand the process I go through when deciding whether I'm truly interested in a guy. I consider myself in a phase of "pre-dating," which is that time between the moment I meet a guy and the moment I feel like we've seen each other enough to consider ourselves "dating." Within the period of pre-dating, I've been able to identify three stages of my growing desire to date a guy: attraction, curiosity, and interest.

As it was with Jonathan, my initial attraction can occur in the first split second I see a guy or it can pop up sometime in the middle of our first date. A smile, a posture, a humorous or sarcastic remark about my need to wear high-heeled shoes, a gesture of empathy toward homeless people or crying puppies, or a quirky, shared moment will trigger the "spark" that makes me slightly tilt my head as I think, *I really dig that about him.*

No matter my level of attraction, I eventually engage in a small internal debate. I'm calling that my "curiosity stage," when I begin assessing a guy's genuine likability factor as I analyze a series of questions. *Is he really as interesting as he seems?*

Is there anything remarkable about him? Are there any immediate red flags?

In the past, I don't think I've invested enough time in the curiosity phase. Instead of using diligent discernment to figure out if a guy is worth my time, I jump straight to my third stage of desire: interest. I'm starting to realize how important it is to use serious judgment during pre-dating.

Going out on a bunch of first dates has helped me identify whether I genuinely like a guy or am only feigning interest because he seems to be the only man with a pulse giving me attention. I'm feeling more empowered as I gauge comparisons and evaluate who could be compatible with me. And I can use the art of wise judgment without being a cruel person.

For instance, I'm aware of my growing curiosity about Evan. I spend a lot of time thinking about him and wondering what he's like, what he's doing, and whether he likes me. I was happy when I found another excuse to email him. "I think your sister commented on my blog," I wrote. Did he understand what I really meant: *I've been thinking about you. Are you thinking of me, too?* The more we chat over email, the more I can tell that my curiosity is turning into genuine interest in moving from pre-dating to dating. But I have ten more dates to go, and several other men who register the same intimate focus. Today is simply an Evan day.

As I start to realize which guys pique my romantic attraction, I find that I'm having a familiar conversation over and over with my girlfriends. Earlier in the day, Elena sat in my office, sipping on a cup of coffee as we dished about the guys I'd gone out with so far.

"So, who do you think you like the most?" she asked, sitting down and clutching her coffee cup.

"Definitely *Jon-a-than*," I said, musically stretching out each syllable of his name. "He's to die for. But I also still really dig Evan." I laughed. "Oh! Wait! And Adam, Allen, Jared, and Christian," I said, ticking them off on my fingers. I was a mess of giggles. "I really can't believe how great they all are."

"Lucky! So what about the other guys? What's wrong with *them?*"

"There's nothing *wrong* with them," I said. "They're all incredible guys. But they just don't seem to fit as *my* guy, you know? It's not like I'm gonna end up dating a bunch of guys at once in *real life*, right?"

This is not exactly the mental or emotional situation I had imagined I would find myself in once I started this whole project. I figured I would learn *something* and maybe find some of the guys interesting. But did I really expect to be two-thirds through my project and feeling curious about half a dozen guys? It was a literal smorgasbord of compatibility.

"Well, hopefully you'll get to add Kevin to your long list of lovers tonight," she said, winking.

I shared my theories about my pre-dating stages with Kevin, at a Creole restaurant in Midtown. While picking at my shrimp gumbo and macaroni and cheese, I realized that the two of us were kindred spirits. It had me wondering, *how could*

I have been missing someone so much like me when he was right in front of me every day?

Before our date, I knew Kevin vaguely. We work in the same building and have mutual friends. We had exchanged a few emails regarding business, but I knew nothing about him other than the fact that Elena raved about how nice he was.

We had met up a few hours earlier outside the Ed Sullivan Theater, and it felt a little strange for me at first. I had adjusted to meeting complete strangers. But I had seen Kevin's face and heard his voice often. I had heard his ideas and knew his reputation as a hard worker. I had to set my preconceived ideas about him aside and avoid assuming I knew him.

Sitting in the audience of *The Late Show with David Letterman* with Kevin was a great experience. We knowingly pointed to the guys in headsets, determined which was the floor director, and debated how well the show was timed.

Kevin's awesome—well-rounded, studied communications at Villanova, worked at a local television affiliate after school, climbed through the ranks of network television—but he suffers from the dreaded "good guy" syndrome.

"Do girls break up with you and say you're too good for them?" I asked during a commercial break.

"Yes!" he exclaimed, pointing to me as if I'd won something. "What is *with* that?"

"You didn't make it through the curiosity stage, eh?"

"I guess not."

"It happens," I said, shaking my head. "They don't know what they're missing."

He looked at me with one of those *Yeah, right!* expressions.

"I don't get it," he said, shaking his head. "I take a girl out. We have fun. And then after a few dates she says I'm not *egdy* enough."

Now it was time for me to roll my eyes. "Well, do you even *want* to be edgy?"

"No. But I know how to have a good time. I go out. What do they *want?*"

"I think they want to keep having a good time, but maybe their idea of a good time is just different than yours."

"Yeah, maybe," he said. And for a moment, he looked at me, as if asking something he couldn't bring himself to say.

"Seriously, Kevin," I reassured him. "These women don't know what they're missing."

And they don't—even me, I realized. Because here I was, feeling more like an advocate for him than a *possibility*. I was the example in action. Because while I thought he was cool, fun, and interesting, I felt more like like a friend than a potential lover.

Which is hard to figure out, because he's so fun. He goes out nearly every night. He sings, acts . . . loves music, movies, concerts, and plays. Basically, he's a Renaissance man who's been dating progressive women. And all the women who have similar interests quickly become his friends. Like me.

As we sat through the taping, comfortable together, we kept interrupting each other excitedly, talking about our favorite shows, books, movies. We promised to exchange our copies of must-reads and agreed to call if we ever needed a buddy for a Friday night movie.

As for dating, Kevin has his own rules, too.

"I'm no longer saying 'one and done.'"

"Like—as in one, night stands?" I asked, nearly choking on my words.

"No!" he laughed. "I mean *one date* and then done. I've decided I've gotta' start going out on more second dates."

"That's exactly what I think," I said excitedly. "In the past, I've decided too quickly whether things will work out with a guy or not. And I've ended up writing off some pretty great guys. I'm so dumb."

"I think that's normal," he said.

"Yeah, but then I sit around and bitch about guys' not asking me out. And then I fall for the next dud who pays attention to me. Such a vicious cycle I've created. But I think I'm *finally* starting to realize the importance of just relaxing a bit, giving guys a chance, and allowing attraction to happen when it happens. I think I just need to respect the beginning stages a little more than I have."

"I think I've put too much emphasis on *sparks,*" he said.

"Yes!" I said, taking my turn to point at him. "I'm like that, too!"

"If there aren't any sparks, I've *gotta* give it a chance, even if we just become friends."

"Well, most of the people we date, we won't end up marrying, right? I mean, I consider myself having a one hundred percent failure rate so far."

"A *failure?*" he asked.

"I'm just saying that all of the men I've dated haven't ended up staying around forever. I'm not saying I didn't learn anything or that the time I spent with them wasn't worth it. But the more I look at potential dates as future friends, the less pressure I put on guys as hopefully being *The One*," I said, flashing my fingers in quotation marks. "It eases the pressure a bit."

"But what happens if someone *is* The One?" he asked.

"Then I guess it's a good thing I'm starting to be more patient during pre-dating," I said, smiling. "Maybe I won't let a good guy sneak by as easily as I used to."

"That's exactly why I think second—even third—dates are so important. I'm willing to take time and give things a chance."

"Kevin," I said, lifting an eyebrow, "do you think of yourself as a romantic?"

He nodded. "I guess so."

"I think I might be, too," I said, debating in my head whether the statement was true.

He had a quizzical look on his face. "Maybe that's why some girls think I'm not edgy enough."

"Maybe," I said. And then I settled back in my seat to enjoy the rest of my gumbo.

DATE 20: COLLIN

Subject: New York Post interview?

Hi Tamara,

I'm very interested in writing an article about your blog, which many, many
of my friends are reading religiously.
I was thinking it could be a perfect
Sunday pre–Valentine's Day feature. If
you're interested, drop me a line and
we can chat.

The project was beginning to feel bigger than I
intended. I kept thinking it was all about learning how to
connect better with men and figure out what I was doing wrong
when it came to dating. But as I read the email request from the
New York Post, I felt that same sinking feeling in my stomach
that I did when I emailed Diane Sawyer. *Am I really ready to*

have my dating debacles publicized for all of America? Can my insecurities handle all the judgment that might come my way?

My mind was still mulling over the inquiry from the *Post* when I met up with my date Collin, a guy who seemed happily above insecurities because he's the type of person who wholeheartedly embraces risks and doesn't mind embarrassing himself. Or at least that was my impression.

I'd known Collin for a few months and still hadn't managed to figure him out. He was a friendly, fun, and artsy filmmaker, willing to try anything. He'd contacted me a few days ago, wondering when *he* would get his chance to be part of the project.

He was joyfully fearless and always had a smile on his face.

But he was also a bit, well, *odd.* He had something unlike anyone else I'd ever met—an alter ego.

He often spoke of his alien counterpart, Zantar, who regularly appeared as the star in Collin's films: Zantar dressed as Santa. Zantar falling in love. Zombie Zantar. You get the picture. And Collin frequently spoke candidly about Zantar as if he were his roommate, existing alive and well somewhere and constantly in his presence.

When I first heard about Zantar's existence, I thought Collin was crazy. Seriously. But I desperately wanted to know more about him. Who, exactly, *was* Zantar? Did Collin actually believe Zantar was real?

When we arrived at Collin's favorite taco spot in Spanish Harlem, he was content and smiling, just as always. He had dark good looks, and an average build, and dressed like a man who worked in a bookstore—loafers, faded jeans, and a nappy sweater over a faded concert T-shirt. He did *not* look nutty. More like a "regular guy" who might like comic books.

"You look lovely," he said, reaching to open the door for me.

"Thank you," I said, feeling genuinely uplifted by his sentiment. I was sure I wore my tired dishevelment on my sleeve—almost literally. Admittedly, his kind flattery gave me a boost. I absentmindedly brushed invisible wrinkles out of my top and smiled.

Collin's taco joint resembled something he would find back in his home state of California. The diner was dimly lit, with a refurbished jukebox outlined with pulsing pink neon lights. The walls were hung with crooked paintings of men in sombreros serenading young señoritas. In the corner, a big television blared Spanish telenovelas. When we entered, a loud bell jingled, grabbing the attention of the restaurant owner, who stood by the cash register, engrossed in the melodrama beaming from the television. She grabbed a couple of menus and bustled over to welcome us, recognizing Collin. *"Hola!"* she cheered, smiling and reaching her arms wide to give him a hug.

"Hola!" he said joyfully with a sharp American accent. They chitchatted happily as we settled in at a Formica table that looked like it had been there since the 1950s.

Collin did his best to order for both of us in Spanish, telling her I'd like the *burrito de frijoles y queso*. He sat tall and stroked his finger down the menu. *"Para mi?"* he asked brightly, *"Para mi, los tacos de pollo."*

I could understand what the two were saying, but I couldn't figure out how to speak Spanish for myself. Kind of like when I can look at someone else's relationship and quickly rattle off all their problems, but it's harder to find the right thoughts or words to describe what's going wrong in my own life. I uttered the only word I felt comfortable saying correctly: *"Gracias."*

"Other than the fact that this place is quite tasty," Collin said, "I just like its delightful atmosphere."

Delightful. *Who uses words like that?*

Everything about Collin exudes "artist." He's a gentle soul—poetic, even—who seems to infuse everything with creative nuance. From his hip dark-framed glasses to his spiky hair to his cool canvas messenger bag—even to his alien friend.

"What does Zantar think of this place?" I asked, probing for an entry into his thoughts on his elfish friend. Frankly, I felt a little nosy asking about Zantar, but I wanted the dirt on him. I'd known Collin just well enough to know any line of questioning wouldn't lead down a *totally* kooky path. He'd never actually shifted into the Zantar persona anywhere other than on camera—at least as far as I'd known. There wasn't really a chance I'd spend the rest of the night on a date with an alien. *Was there?*

"Oh," he said kindly, "he loves tacos."

I hesitated with my next question but felt weirdly compelled to see where this would go. "Ummm, where, exactly, did Zantar *come* from?"

"Zantar?" he asked. "Zantar's traveled a long way to get to Earth. But he loves to spend time here." Collin spoke lovingly and seriously about Zantar, as if he were more than just an imaginary friend. He knew every detail about Zantar's home planet. His dietary needs. His likes and dislikes. But Collin and his alien alter ego were never in the same place at the same time, although they're obviously friends with similar tendencies.

As I looked more closely at Collin's dark hair, piercing blue eyes, handsome chiseled face, and cute glasses, I started to realize that Collin could very well be Clark Kent. And Zantar was his Superman.

I could remember wanting to be a superhero when I was little. I would dress in Wonder Woman underwear, pile pillows high onto the couch, climb to the top, and jump to the ground, pretending I could fly. As Wonder Woman, I could do anything. I was beautiful. I had superhuman strength. I could fight for myself and would win every time. Wonder Woman had everything, including a cool invisible plane.

In a way, Zantar was a superhero who would help Collin do anything. Not only was he Collin's creative outlet, but he was also Collin's excuse to act kooky. When Collin created his films and then acted in them, as Zantar, he identified himself as Collin in the credits solely as director and producer. With a malleable character in his films, Collin could push his creativity to the limit and take full control of his craft. If his films were a success, Collin could take the credit. If they failed, Zantar could be the one to blame. Of course, lest you think Collin was a functioning psychotic, he knew Zantar wasn't an actual living, breathing being. He was simply a muse for Collin's creativity.

I started to realize that rather than nutty, Collin might, in fact, be artistically brilliant. He began to seem less weird and more intriguing.

As we talked more, I learned that Collin had studied film and moved to New York City to pursue his dreams in the movie-making industry. He grew up reading comic books, adventure tales, and anything else he could get his hands on. In his tote bag, he carried a few books from the library, including a gigantic biography of Abraham Lincoln. He was quirky, esoteric. I liked his multifaceted personality. Life with someone like Collin would certainly never be boring, but it might not ever be conventional as well—and even though I consider myself a creative and open-minded person, I gravitate a little more toward the balance and security of conventionality. Still, I was thoroughly enjoying our time tonight.

"Where'd you learn Spanish?" I asked, taking a bite of my *muy bueno* burrito.

"I studied it in school and spent a month in Chile. I don't know much, but I like to pick up words for practice."

"I've always wanted to learn Spanish," I said. And I meant it. I really did.

"Let's begin, then!" he announced, sitting up in his most tutorial posture. He started listing off items in the room: *vaso* for "cup," *plato* for "plate," and *delicioso* to describe his love for the taco. Collin was an entertaining cross between a class clown and a funny old grandpa.

"You're a good teacher," I said, laughing.

"Aww, thank you. I actually teach English to Spanish speakers."

"You *do?*" I asked, surprised that Collin was less alien and more human the more we spoke. Apparently he was a superhero not only for himself, but for other people too.

"When do you get *time?*"

"I make time."

The more I learned about him, the more I wanted to *be* like him. He has a carefree sense about life, he's genuine, and he's friendly to everyone around him. He's found his inner superhero. And most of all, he isn't afraid of being different. He isn't afraid of who he is.

More lessons.

I hopped on the bus after our date and wondered if I could ever be as brave or creative as Collin. *Is there a superhero hiding within me?*

Just then I spotted a handsome man with flawless chocolate skin and dark, inviting eyes. I felt my cheeks blush as he caught my gaze and smiled. *Am I brave enough to talk to him? Do I dare ask him to be one of my thirty-one dates?*

I imagined myself searching for *my* inner superhero. Like Diana Prince, I would become Wonder Woman. I would spin in circles like a small tornado and transform into an all-powerful, brave, and beautiful Amazon wearing thick gold bracelets and a perfectly slimming uniform. I would whip my lasso, latching on to the handsome stranger and luring him my way. I would draw him close with the most brief, seductive eye contact. And just as I felt the power of my all-consuming alter ego, the bus slowed down and he stood up, walking past me toward the door.

"Have a good night," he said, smiling.

I heard his soft voice echo in my head as I watched him leave.

I am no Wonder Woman yet. But I can feel her strength starting to spin like a cyclone within me.

That night, I responded to the *New York Post* interviewer. "Yes," I said. "I am willing."

DATE 21:
JUAN-CARLOS

I'd always heard that it takes twenty-one days to develop a new habit. So what had three weeks of nonstop dating done for me? Had I become a kinder, more vulnerable, and less judgmental person when meeting a man? Had I gained confidence? With ten days left, I figured nothing could surprise me, but sure enough, every man had his own endearing quirks.

Juan-Carlos was a handsome high school math teacher who dressed like a stockbroker and loved good music. I first saw him standing outside New York University's Black Box Theatre, wearing a long, well-tailored trench coat and holding a small bag of Godiva chocolates.

"Juan-Carlos?" I said as I approached him.

"My friends call me J.C.," he said, handing me the chocolates. "I hope you like chocolate."

"Ninety percent of my diet is chocolate," I said confidently. I felt like I was finally starting to hit my stride with these dates, maybe feeling a little residue from the superhero charms of the night before. Or maybe it was because I was two-thirds of the way through my project and could feel the finish line nearing.

Inside the small, dark venue, we watched a free series of piano performances featuring classics from Chopin and Beethoven and a few original student works. I looked around at the audience and noticed something unusual. I felt as if the last twenty-one days had helped me look not only at men more lovingly, but at *all* people.

How is this possible?

I felt gratitude for the woman behind the piano, who delicately danced her fingers across the keys, sharing her inner passion via music. It was as if there were a surging energy of love pulsing from the piano. I felt it in my bones, in my feet, in my heart. The room was a wellspring of intense but positive emotion. A man in the front row sat forward, watching proudly. An older couple sat beside him holding hands, the husband dozing off as the slow, soft rhythms lulled him to sleep. Watching each person somehow made me feel connected with—and grateful for—everyone.

And yet, coupled with this overwhelming feeling of love for humanity, I noticed, too, a surge of sadness. I had come so far in my project, and yet somehow I felt like a failure. *Am I really learning anything from all this? What happened to channeling Wonder Woman?* I was confused by how much my confidence vacillated from one date to another. Some days I felt like I was on the right track, and other days I felt a rush of existential angst: *What am doing? What's the purpose? Is this just a big show, a selfish indulgence?* Somehow, something deeper was missing—something meaningful. I vowed to keep my chin up and a lasso at my side.

After the final bow, J.C. suggested we stop into a neighborhood favorite, Cozy Soup 'n' Burger. I wanted to try its famous split pea soup and some hot chocolate. Comfort food was a good call for this night. I was looking forward to settling down and getting to know J.C., whose calm demeanor complemented my mood.

Juan-Carlos ordered a sandwich and sipped on a cup of peppermint tea.

"After a long day teaching math to junior high and high school students, it's nice to relax with some soft music and a warm cup of tea," he said.

"I've always heard that music and math go well together," I said. "If you're good in one, it can actually help strengthen your skills in the other."

"Well, I do love both."

We sipped our hot drinks, feeling cozy, and I asked him about his job. I was surprised, intrigued, and humbled by his inverse road to become a teacher. Before landing as a math teacher at a private school in Brooklyn, he'd graduated magna cum laude from the University of Pennsylvania and turned down a six-figure job on Wall Street.

"My mom raised me by herself and urged me to work hard," he said. "That led me to a good high school, and that's where I met a really great mentor who was an incredible influence on me. It made me really want to teach and try to help others."

"That's incredible," I said, amazed by his tender heart. "I tend to believe it takes an *extremely* patient person to teach junior high and high school kids." And then I realized Juan-Carlos wasn't just patient. He was pretty much a saint.

In the middle of explaining what he loves about teaching, he interrupted himself. "Excuse me for a second." He bowed his head and clasped his hands. I watched his brown eyes close delicately and the corners of his mouth lift into a slight smile.

Is he PRAYING? On a DATE? I looked around at the other patrons, wondering if they were watching me watch him. I wasn't sure how to react. I'd never had anyone pray on a date before. I felt self-conscious, even a little uncomfortable. I didn't like that I felt that way. The praying seemed to go on longer than necessary. I also didn't like that I even *cared* about that. Where had my earlier graciousness toward humanity fled?

He lifted his head back up and smiled, as if refreshed. "Thanks."

I shrugged nonchalantly, dipping my spoon into the soup, pretending not to care. "Sure."

His prayer didn't just have me wondering about him—praying in public is unusual, right?—it had me wondering about myself. *How can I claim to be a spiritual God-and people-loving person and then sit here and judge him for not being afraid of showing his faith?* I was a hypocrite. I tried to readjust my attitude.

"Soooo," I said, searching for the right words, "are you religious?"

"I am," he said, happily chewing his sandwich.

"Christian? Catholic?"

"Catholic," he said. "Raised Catholic. My mom's from Colombia—best Catholic out there. But," he said, smiling, "it's okay if *you're* not Catholic, Tamara. I think it's really important to be open-minded."

"Absolutely. I totally agree," I said emphatically. *So then why have I been such a judgy jerk about his praying?* "I don't think I really know too many people who pray in public."

"I didn't always," he said. "But then I met a guy in college who I *really* respected. Just this great guy. Nice to everybody. Really smart. Had lots of friends. And one time when we were all with a big group out to eat, he stopped for a second to say a silent prayer, and it really made an impact on me. I thought, *If he can do that, why don't I?* So I have. Ever since. And I think it's important to pray."

"I *pray*," I said, sounding defensive. "But I just never really think to do it in public. Makes me feel uncomfortable." *Geez! What is wrong with me?* It was like I was challenging him. Maybe I was really just challenging myself.

"It used to make me uncomfortable, too," he said. "But I just figured, why not?"

He was right—about the "why not." About living your *own* values, whether they're religious or not. I had always been someone who wasn't showy about my beliefs—mostly because my beliefs changed so often. And I'd always been wary of people who appeared earnest and condescending about their religion. But Juan-Carlos seemed to have the right balance: He was unapologetic about his faith and wasn't judgmental of mine.

And then I realized something. He goes by "J.C."—as in Jesus Christ. Could Juan-Carlos, in some way, actually be in my life to bring some message from God?

I started to remember the moments of sadness I'd had earlier on the date, the doubts I'd had about learning anything new or changing my habits. Without even trying, Juan-Carlos was teaching me about kindness and tolerance.

"Juan-Carlos," I said matter-of-factly, "you're a really good guy."

He looked at me with an innocent, youthful blush. "Thank you. What brought that on?"

"You just seem like a really good dude. You help kids, you love your mom, you pray in public."

"Well, that's about as public as I get. I'm actually pretty private. About most things. In fact," he paused, looking back and forth between me and his plate, "I *really* wasn't sure about coming tonight."

"Oh yeah?" I said with surprise. "Why not?"

"Wellll," he said, "I thought about it a *lot*. And, I mean, when I first got the email from my friend about it, I was like, 'No way. Absolutely not.' I mean, I figured I'd get nervous, and I wasn't so sure how comfortable I would be, and you were writing about it and everything."

"So, what made you change your mind?" I was humbled by his candor and his readiness to reveal his insecurity. *I thought all guys were confident,* I thought, *and I the only one who's a mess of emotional contradictions.*

He thought for a few seconds. "You know, I really don't know," he said, smiling the whole time. "I guess I just figured it was gonna be worth it for some reason. I mean, I really thought it would be good for me. I could grow from this experience. Live in the present. Trust the timing. See what happens. And whoever reads whatever you write, then I'm gonna be okay with that."

I was stunned. That was *me*, that was *my* boilerplate for this project. Did all my other dates, despite their confidence, poise, and charm, feel the same way? And certainly, I hoped he meant what he said about not caring what people read about the project, because I had an admission to make, and this was the perfect time to do so.

"Well then," I said, nervously awaiting his response, "I guess this is when I should tell you that I'm meeting with the *New York Post* tomorrow."

He laughed in surprise. "You're *what?!*" He shook his head and tried his best to compose himself. "Are you being serious? No, you're kidding. Are you? Wait, are you *serious?*"

"I am," I said, laughing along with him. "So, will you be okay with that? With, like, the possibility of a lot of people reading about you?"

"You know what?" he said, placing his hands firmly on the table and his face showing an ever-growing smile. "It's gonna be okay. Okay. Yes. This is good."

"Are you sure?"

"Absolutely."

"Oh, good," I said. "Because I'm also going to be on *Good Morning America* in a few days."

He burst into laughter. "Are you serious? *Are* you serious? Oh, I can't believe this!"

"Are you okay with all this?"

"You know what? I *am*. I am. Wow, that's crazy. I mean, you never really know what you're getting yourself into, do you?"

And he was right. When I started this project, I had no idea what I was getting myself into. Frankly, I'm still not sure, but I'm on the right course. I can *feel* that, even under the roller coaster of emotions—going from insecure to confident to insecure again. One thing is certain, though, and that's that I am learning *something* from each of these men, and the risk is not mine alone—it's theirs as well.

In our few hours together, I felt an easy friendship growing with J.C. He was much more complex than just the "music-loving, math-teaching, prays-in public handsome Colombian" I made him out to be. He wanted to pursue his PhD. He thought his mother was the most respectable woman in the world. He believed in magic, and love. He even read my palm, gazing at the deep, old-lady lines in my hand, deducting that a "long-lasting love" would unleash itself in my life.

He looked at his watch and stared in amazement. "I can't believe we've been talking this long!"

"Oh, I'm so sorry," I said. "You need to get up early, don't you?"

"No, no, no," he explained. "I just can't believe so much *time* has gone by and there is still so much I want us to talk about!"

He was a lovely, kind man, and he had in fact made me feel some sort of assurance from the heavens. Somehow I knew I would come out of the project being a better person, just because I had been blessed with meeting men like him. My project wasn't just helping me have more faith in men or mankind. What I was finally gaining was faith in myself.

I was ready to tackle tomorrow's newspaper interview. And I didn't even need a superhero costume to do it.

DATE 22: DEREK

Ten years ago, Derek flipped a coin, deciding his fate to move to New York instead of Kansas City. I can imagine his younger self staring down at the silvery profile of George Washington, scared and hopeful about whatever his future held. That image stayed in my head as I started to remember something important: There are two sides to every coin.

When we chatted over email to schedule our date, Derek seemed like a cool, normal guy:

> I'll be in New York "uniform" with blue
> jeans and a black leather jacket. I'm
> about 6'2", 175 pounds, a shaved head
> with a beard. Unfortunately I could
> look like a lot of people.

He seemed really intrigued by my project, and he didn't even seem to mind when I asked if it would be okay for a photographer from the *New York Post* to tag along and take some pictures of our date. I figured the photographer would witness a fun night. I was wrong.

Derek and I planned to meet a few blocks from a free outdoor snowboarding event, which brought in a six-story-tall downhill slope covered in fake snow for snowboarders to drop into a half pipe. Some of the world's best snowboarders, and thousands of New Yorkers, would be there. It must have been one of the coldest nights of the year, and when we met for the first time, Derek seemed equally cold in his demeanor.

I noticed his shaved head and leather jacket and walked toward him. "Derek?"

"Oh, hey," he said nonchalantly, nodding to acknowledge my presence. He was not in the least bit enthusiastic, nor did he seem very interested in meeting me. Without so much as a "how do you do," he said, "Let's go," and we followed a crowd funneling toward the snowboarding event.

Where's the nice, cool guy I was expecting?

To cut the silence and his awkward dismissiveness, I asked generic get-to-know-you questions, hoping to find—if not some sort of emotional response—at least some common ground.

"So, what do you do for work?" I asked, as we shouldered past people crowding toward the stadium, waiting for the event to start.

He shrugged, keeping his gaze forward. "I'm just a personal trainer."

"Oh, really? How'd you get into that?"

"I guess I fell into it. I didn't plan on it."

Is this going to be one of those dates when I spend the evening interviewing him? "What'd you want to do instead?"

"A bunch of stuff. But I only went to college for a year and a half. Dropped out."

"Oh," I said, feeling as if he had already decided I was a waste of his time. I looked around to see if any of the strangers passing by us could somehow sense my boredom. "So," I said, trying to keep a conversation—any conversation—going, "where'd you grow up?"

"Northern Virginia."

"Me too!" I exclaimed, thinking he would be equally surprised to learn not only that we were from the same region but also that he went to one of my rival high schools. But no. He just kept looking forward, nodding, as if my presence were bothering him.

Over email he seemed so much more interested in getting to know me, I thought. *Why the switch?*

I felt resentment creep up inside me, even annoyance. I looked closely at his thin beard outlining his jaw. *Why does he have it shaved like that?* I wondered, feeling pissy. *And why the shaved-head look? I don't get it.*

The snowboarding event was much more packed than we'd expected. It was as if an entire sports stadium full of people had been compacted and dumped into a tiny space on the East River and everyone was shoving their way to the front. I tried to squeeze my way past the crowd toward a clearing in the street, but I was pushed and shoved by loud teens and angry college students blocking my way.

This date sucks. Why did I suggest this in the first place?

I inched my way out of the mass of people just as the *New York Post* photographer, Allison, arrived. I felt like she was my rescue crew coming to drag me back into the world of nicer people. But my relief was a mixed bag. She'd certainly sense our total lack of a connection—and if she didn't, the camera would reveal it.

Derek looked back at the dense crowd funneling toward the snowboarding event. He suddenly spoke up loudly over the roar, startling me. "Do you want to go somewhere else?" he asked, motioning away from the madness.

I nodded, and as we walked away, I deliberated an escape. *My rules say I need to last only thirty-one minutes. Then I can bail. I can just tell him, "This isn't working for me," or I could say I forgot about something I had to do. But how in the world am I gonna pull that off? In front of a photographer? Isn't she supposed to be telling the story of how "awesome" all my dates are?* I was trapped.

Once again, Derek's gaze was directed ahead of him, but his tone started to soften. "We can go play pool if you want. There's a really good place not too far from here. I think it'd be fun."

Fun? I imagined the pool parlor as a dark, seedy, cramped pub with smoke curling in the air. But I figured it couldn't be much worse than standing outside. Could it?

My toes started to feel more tender with every step we took. I tugged at my winter coat, pulling it in for warmth. But the rough wind seemed to seep through the fabric as it slapped against my skin. *Coldest. Date. Ever.* I turned back and glanced at Allison, who was following us, and rolled my eyes. Could she tell our date wasn't going well?

"Are we almost *there?*" I whined, just as I would on a long, arduous road trip with my parents.

He looked at me with kind eyes and patted me gently on the shoulder. "We're almost there. I promise it'll be worth it." His tone caught me off guard. He suddenly seemed less abrasive. *Why was he such a jerk before and now he's trying to play nice?*

I mulled over my confusion and had to swallow my pride a bit. If I was going to make my way through the rest of the evening, I needed a serious attitude adjustment. That was a tall order—one that only God could fill. I sighed softly and said a quick prayer in my head, thinking of Juan-Carlos's kindness and example: *Please help me pay attention to the good in this guy.*

And then something happened that had never occurred before in my life. In an *instant,* my prayer was answered. Quicker than a snap, I decided to stop being a brat and started listening instead. I was amazed at how my attitude flipped from annoyed to impressed as Derek shared a little more about his life.

"I'm hoping this is the year my business partner and I finally get to open up our new bar," he said, smiling with passion, completely unaffected by the cold air buffeting us as we walked. "Any day now, we're supposed to get the architectural mock-up. So everything's *finally* coming together. And I've been *racking* my brain for a name," he said, shaking his fist, mimicking his frustration.

Derek started to appear more dynamic than before. "So, you're not *just* a personal trainer like you said?" I asked.

"Yeah, I've got some businesses going on the side. But mostly I spend time with clients, helping them achieve their goals."

"But you work out, too, right?"

"Yeah, I do some races."

"Like marathons?"

"Kind of. Do you know what an Ironman competition is?"

I stopped walking, and for a second I forgot I was freezing. Was Derek telling me, casually, that he had completed what I considered the ultimate physical challenge? The Ironman is a daylong race of consecutive events that included a two-and-a-half-mile swim, followed by a 112-mile bike ride, then a quick change into running shoes for a full marathon—26.2 miles. And did I mention it's a race? No stopping, no resting, no losing precious time.

"You've completed an *Ironman?*" My jaw was squarely on the ground.

He shrugged, as if it were no big deal. "Yeah, my friend convinced me it was this incredible experience. But it *sucked*. I *hated* it. And everybody else who'd done it before loved it. I mean, was I missing something? Like, did I do it wrong? I didn't get it. So I tried it again."

"You did an Ironman *twice?*"

"I had to see if I would love it the second time."

"Did you?" I asked, my eyes widening in continued shock.

"No," he laughed, "it was *worse*."

Is he actually impressing me? "You think you'd ever do another one?"

"Yeah, I think I'll keep doing them until I'm happy with my time."

I felt as if I were spending the evening with Dr. Jekyll and Mr. Awesome. How was a guy who had started out seeming like he could be the worst date of this project starting to seem so dynamic?

When we arrived at the billiard club, it was far from the seedy dive I had imagined. It was a vast space with high ceilings, lots of windows, and dozens of college students hanging out by the bar or playing pool. Derek was right. It could be fun.

Soon after racking the balls, Derek scratched on the eight ball, sending me into quick victory. We reracked and I started to realize that I felt a little nervous about whether he would judge me by my poor pool playing. Wait a minute. Did I actually *want* Derek to like me?

"Tamara," he said, laughing, "the girlie stance with the feet together is cute, but it's not helping much with your shots." He walked toward me and showed me how to take a better "man stance," standing with his legs shoulder-width apart and bending his knees a little. "You got it?" he asked.

"I think so," I said. I might have *looked* more like a pool player, but I'm not sure how much actual improvement there was. I crouched down in man stance, leaned over the table, carefully aimed my stick at the cue ball, and thrust with a quick force. The white ball clanked two stripe balls into the corner pocket.

"Nice shot!" he cheered.

"Helps to have a good trainer," I said, my smile growing so wide it hurt my cheeks. I was having so much fun, it wasn't until Allison, the photographer, said goodbye that I realized she'd been nearby the whole time.

After our time at the tables was up, Derek and I headed to a nearby coffee shop to just sit and talk.

"Have your dates all been okay so far?" he asked.

"Pretty much."

"Really? Would you go out with any of them again?"

"I would," I admitted. "Which is crazy, because I totally didn't think this project would lead to me meeting any guys I'd be interested in. And it's not like I'm interested in becoming every guy's *girlfriend*. I mean, I'll go out on a second date with one of the guys for my thirty-first date. Then maybe go out with a few others after that. See what happens."

"All the dates really went *that* well?"

"Yeah. I mean, it's not like they're all perfect. And I'm not romantically attracted to *all* of them. But I'd at least try a second date. And with some guys—yeah, I'd probably wanna see them more." I couldn't help but wonder if he was fishing here a little. We definitely were more comfortable together. In fact, I could feel myself becoming more flirty, feeling a bit of a spark. I tried to keep my cool, especially while talking about other guys.

"About how many of the guys would you say you liked a lot?" he asked.

"About a third."

"A *third?* The dates were that good, huh?"

"Well," I explained, "it's not like all the dates were great right from the start. Some start out rocky, but then they get better."

"You mean, like our date."

I bit my lower lip, trying to hide my embarrassed smile. "Yes, exactly." We were being real with each other. "So—what was *up* with that?"

"Honestly? I read up on all your other dates last night."

"Oh yeah?" I said, wondering what he'd read that made him act like a jerk. Had I said something offensive in my blog posts? "And what'd you think?"

He laughed. "There's no *way* there are *that* many good guys out there. I mean, let's break it down," he said, counting on his fingers. "One guy helps the homeless on Christmas. There's a brain doctor or something. A guy who helps sick puppies. How does anybody compete?"

I laughed. "Yeah, I can see that."

"They're all surgeons and fighter pilots."

"What do you mean?"

"A couple summers ago my buddy and I were both going out with these girls. Went out for a while. And then we *both* got dumped for other guys. He got dumped for a fighter pilot. I got showed up by a surgeon. So I called him up last night after reading your blog and was like, 'Guess what? All these guys she's going out with? Surgeons and fighter pilots!'"

I laughed. "Derek! You can't let that stuff intimidate you."

"So I figured, 'I'm just gonna go out there and I'm gonna be the *regular guy.*'"

"But Derek," I reasoned, "*why* do you think all these guys come across as so great?"

"I dunno. Either you're an amazing writer or you somehow *really* lucked out with the best New York has to offer."

I shook my head. "No, it's neither of those. It's because I've been doing my best to try and see the *best* in those guys—to see who they really are. I mean, c'mon. Like, let's look at you, 'regular guy.' You completed two Ironman competitions. I'm sorry, Derek. You're no *regular guy,* no matter how hard you try."

Derek was impressing me. He was a self-made man whose life took many unexpected turns. When he dropped out of college, Derek was set to enlist in the navy. A couple weeks before he was supposed to report to duty, he fell three stories from a balcony.

"Were you drunk?" I asked.

"Are you *crazy?*" he asked. "Of *course* I was drunk. Who drops three stories from a balcony when they're not drunk?"

"True."

"So after I fell I was laid up for a while. Broke my jaw and," he paused as he pointed out the next injury, "my right index finger." He wiggled it meaningfully. "Trigger finger. So, no navy for me."

Then, after that, his father passed away unexpectedly, leaving him, his mother, and two sisters behind. "I'd always had a pretty good relationship with them, but when my dad died, it really pulled me and my mom and my sisters together."

It was so illuminating to see how much an impression of someone could change in mere hours. Derek had a great sense of self, which drew me to him. I felt comfortable around him and started to see him in a completely different way. His beard no longer seemed silly but *fitting*, empowering, and attractive. I had gone from dreading the date to feeling a nice connection, wishing time weren't ticking away so quickly. I'd finally begun really *liking* him. I wanted to start our date all over, take back all the moments I'd wasted throwing a mental tantrum, and wished I could just talk with him all night. But the clock crept toward midnight, and it was time to go home and sleep a few hours.

"I've really gotta get going," I said. "Tomorrow morning's an early start for me." I bit my lip in nervous response as I thought about the early-morning television appearance that awaited me.

"Well," he said, "no matter what happens with your project—whether we go out for your thirty-first date or whatever—I hope I get to see you again."

"Me too," I said, surprised by the turn the evening had taken. I had begun the night thinking we would hate each other. And after only a few hours, I was crushed to be leaving my new crush.

As we walked toward the door to leave, he made one final suggestion. "Between the time we leave this building and when you catch a cab, I guess I still need to save a puppy, help an old lady, and create world peace to match with all the other guys, right?"

"Or maybe you can just keep being the *regular guy.*"

We both laughed, and for a minute I imagined what it might be like to kiss those lips and feel the scratch of his beard. I looked into his eyes for what felt like several minutes, debating whether to make a move, remembering how annoying I had thought he was and how incredibly wrongly I'd judged him. *Does he want to kiss me, too?* I shook it off, hugged him briefly, and said goodnight.

"I hope to see you again," he said.

"Me too," I nodded, registering the truth in my words.

I walked to the subway station, surprised by how much I had grown to like Derek.

The next morning I felt giddy when I found an email from him in my inbox.

Subject: Good Morning

Tamara,

I had a great time last night. I would
love to see you again after you have
completed your project. Hope you have
fun being on TV today and good luck
with the rest of your dates.
-Derek

P.S. I might have come up with a solu-
tion to world hunger as I was walking home last night but didn't write
it down and now I have forgotten it.
Hopefully that's enough to get me in
the category with the fighter pilots and
surgeons. It's the best I can do. There
were no old people to help, no puppies
to save, and I couldn't find anything to
fly. It wasn't a very long walk.

DATE 23: JEREMIAH

I did it. After twelve years of being a behind-the-scenes girl, I made my first appearance on television. My dating project was forcing me to take more risks than I had ever imagined. Not only was I challenging myself to date differently and put my bad habits with men under a microscope, I was also jumping in front of the camera—something I never imagined myself doing throughout my career.

I stood quietly in ABC's busy Times Square studio, shifting my weight from side to side, waiting by dozens of fans from around the country. Each person was vying for a perfect spot to get in front of the camera. Some held poster-boards with greetings written to their families and friends back home. Everyone seemed to be mumbling to each other, creating an orchestrated buzz of urgent energy in the room.

I breathed slowly, reciting assuring mantras in my head. *You won't make an ass out of yourself. You know what you're talking about. It will be over quickly.*

I tried to appear professional, wearing a simple dress and tall boots. But I felt like a little girl dressed up in my mom's clothing. I feigned confidence, standing up straight and smiling widely, just in case anyone looked at me.

The floor director approached me, making sure my microphone was appropriately clipped to the collar of my dress. He talked into a headset, getting a cue for my upcoming segment.

"Okay, Tamara," he said, "I need a mic check. Can you count to five for me?"

I inhaled confidently. "One, two, three—"

"Okay, that's good," he said, and then announced to the entire room, "We're up in thirty seconds!"

The room's volume quieted, and I could hear my heartbeat pulsing heavily in my ears. I started to feel warmer as the bright studio lights beamed on my face. By my side was the beautifully brilliant and poised Diane Sawyer. Next to her was the handsome, hardnosed news attorney Chris Cuomo, whose presence somehow made me think I might not pass out from nervousness. "Tam," he asked, "you ready for this?"

My face tightened in uncertainty. "I guess?"

"You'll do great," he said.

The floor director's voice alerted everyone as his fingers counted down our cue. "Coming out in five, four, three—"

Diane introduced me, waving me on camera, and put her arm around me while asking a simple question. "After all this, what advice do you have for people going out on first dates?"

I felt as if I were having an out-of-body experience, unsure of whose voice was speaking or if I was giving appropriate responses. "First," I said, "don't take first dates too seriously. Second, don't judge too quickly. And third, every guy is somebody's Prince Charming. Maybe not *yours,* but he could be someone *else's.* So respect him."

Diane and Chris wished me luck with the rest of my project as it led toward my pivotal Valentine's Day second date. And then it was over. Three minutes whipped by more quickly than I had imagined. I exhaled a huge sigh, as if I hadn't breathed the whole time I was on camera.

Later that evening, I mulled over my television appearance as I waited at an Indian restaurant for my date, Jeremiah. The smell of curry seemed to be seared into the thick red carpets, and Bollywood music drifted from the bar. It seemed the perfect setting for a man who belonged dancing along the shores of the Ganges. Jeremiah's long, delicate hair fluttered as he rushed into the restaurant, panting and sweating. "I'm so sorry I'm late," he said. "I came as fast as I could from the yoga studio."

He sat down and wiped his forehead, nodding to the bartender. "Vodka tonic, please." He looked at my glass of ice water. "You're not having anything?"

"No. I'm not really a drinker." The date was just getting started, and he was already breaking my no drinking rule. I wasn't quite sure how this was going to work out.

He inhaled slow, long breaths, which was a normal state for him. Jeremiah was a yoga instructor who lived, breathed, and felt every nuance of its philosophies, and his beliefs seemed to spill into every part of his personality. He waved his hair back, resembling the images found on the front of romance novels, and spoke with a breathy lightness. "Right now I'm guiding some workshops based on twelve devotional archetypes."

"You're working on *what?*" I asked, leaning closer as if I hadn't heard him correctly. *This dude might be a weirdo.*

"Archetypes. Our inner characters," he said, floating his hand to his heart. "Each month, we're focusing on different archetypes as we lead people through asanas. Like," he paused, taking a sip of his drink, "have you heard of Lakshmi? Or Rhada?"

I shook my head slowly, not sure of what he was saying.

"Lakshmi is a Hindu goddess—for wealth, prosperity. So we use her as a guide to help people meditate their own good fortune. Rhada," he said, widening his eyes, "she's the essence of infinite beauty, joy, love." He tapped my knee lightly, "You'd be perfect for her."

He talked blissfully for the next several minutes, maybe describing the other archetypes or the history of yoga. I had no idea. He seemed to speak a different language, and I had no idea how to communicate. I just stared, trying to nod every once in a while as if I were digesting everything he said. Finally he grew silent and took another sip.

"Hmm," I said, wondering what to say next. "So, how long have you been practicing yoga?"

"For*ever.*"

"Really?"

"Sort of. My mother taught yoga, so I've been around it my whole life. I've been to India a few times. And I met the

Dalai Lama when I was fifteen," he said, his eyes softening as if in adoration of the memory.

"What was that like?" I asked impressed and curious at the same time. I assumed that for Hindus, meeting the Dalai Lama was analogous to a Christian's meeting Jesus. Whoa.

"It was a life-altering moment for me. Literally. I could feel an entire chakra open," he said, bursting his hands apart, "simply by being in his presence."

I was totally intrigued . . . The truth is, I love anything that seems a little hoodoo-voodoo or earth-loving. Of course, Jeremiah was definitely representing the extreme. But part of me felt this joyous jealousy, wishing I had the passion about anything that Jeremiah does about the world of yoga. Heck, I wish I had the endurance to go to yoga class more than once a year.

"Sounds like it was a great experience for you," I said.

"It was. I'm hoping to go back to India this year, actually. And Berlin. It's beautiful there. And everyone on the streets is smiling. Even the prostitutes seem happy."

"Oh yeah?" I said, laughing in disbelief.

"Not that I got to know any of them well or anything," he explained, his cheeks blushing a little. I liked his gentle, light attitude.

"So, you travel and meditate. You like the journey within—and out?" I asked.

"Isn't that what everything's about? The journey?" he said. I was soaking up everything he said, realizing a lot of it sounded a bit hokey. But I could tell he was being genuine, maybe even a little vulnerable, which I could really appreciate.

"So they say," I said.

"Mm-hmm," he said, taking a look at his empty glass and glancing at his watch. He tensed up, took a second look at his watch, and sounded urgent. "We gotta go!"

"What time is it?" We had planned to stop by an exhibit at the Museum of Modern Art, which closed at eight o'clock.

He hurried to wrap his scarf around his neck. "We only have fifteen minutes!"

We rushed through the street. And in what appeared to be a quick transformation, Jeremiah went from relaxed Zen yoga guru to fast-paced, flustered hunter. He was frazzled and—surprisingly—*funny.*

A guard stood at the door of the MoMA, trying to block anyone from coming in at the last minute. Jeremiah was plotting. "If you kick him in the knees, I'll get him in the eyes!"

Jeremiah bumped past the guard, yelling back at him. "We just want to see the exhibit upstairs!" he yelled, "We'll be quick!"

My heartbeat tried to keep up with my legs' speedy pace as we galloped upstairs to the exhibit on strange love. Jeremiah strained to catch his breath as he pointed to the macabre murals. One depicted the death of two lovers who had hanged themselves. The other was a morbid seduction. Plastered on the wall was the picture of a woman's nude, bloody body. Jeremiah's eyes gaped in embarrassment. "Those were *not* on the website!" he said, in mock modesty.

I loved seeing the lighter side of Jeremiah's personality.

As soon as our breathing mellowed, an announcement blared overhead. "The museum is now *closed.*"

"Well," he said, "shall we walk around the city a bit?"

With every step, Jeremiah seemed to become more complex and lovable.

While yoga was his passion, he also spent many hours a week working as a real estate broker. And he, like most men in their late thirties, had a love for *Star Wars*.

"Plus," he said proudly, "my Yoda impression is spot-on."

"Let's see it," I said, delighted. I'd totally forgotten my weird disconnect with him about yoga and doshas or pranas or whatever.

He tucked his chin, puffed his cheeks, and spoke with a perfect throaty, froggy flair. "Judge me by my size, do you?" he asked, wiggling his face toward mine. "Hmmm? Hmmm?"

Where did this silly side come from? We picked up the pace, nearly skipping with delight toward the massive, gothic St. Patrick's Cathedral, where he announced nonchalantly, "My great-grandfather actually helped build that."

I laughed in amazement. "You are the yin to my yang!"

Jeremiah was a complete enigma: one part seductive and soulful, another part fiery and fearless. I admired that, but it was a little hard to sync with his mercurial persona.

We walked through the grand hall, where reverent echoes bounced off the ceiling. Jeremiah sat in a pew and lowered his voice. "I've been trying to figure out your astrological sign," he said. "Are you into astrology?" he asked.

"I was a long time ago," I said, remembering my phase of New Age curiosity. I'd spent a couple college semesters looking for meaning in my life through astrology, tarot cards, reading auras, anything I could get my hands on. I desperately wanted to be a hippie type, but I felt too boring to meld with their loose sensibilities and appearance: their long peasant skirts, their scent of patchouli. I figured I was too pragmatic. Plus, those ankle-length skirts just wouldn't work for me, since I probably care too much about how I look. And smell.

"Guess my sign," he commanded.

I dug deep into my memory, trying to remember the qualities of each star sign, and gave my best guess. "At first I thought Aquarius," I said, "but now I'm thinking Pisces."

"Cancer," he said. I was way off.

"Okay, what about me? What do you think mine is?" I challenged back.

He squinted his eyes, as if trying to read my mind. "I'm sticking with my original guess. Sagittarius."

"Maybe," I said with a sly smile.

"Maybe? You mean, you don't know?"

"No, I know," I said, laughing. "At least I think I do. See, I thought I was a Sagittarius my whole life. I loved it. Totally part of my identity. And then I had my astrology chart done in college. *Apparently* I'm technically a Capricorn by, like, thirteen minutes."

"Really?" he said, sitting up straight. "I don't believe it."

"Why's that?"

"You just *seem* like a Sagittarius to me."

"How so?"

"They're straightforward. Charming. Risk-takers."

"I'm totally not a risk-taker."

He eyed me quizzically. "Yes. You are," he insisted. "Capricorns are more calculated and goal-oriented."

"I love goals," I said.

"Sagittarians are *brilliant*," he said.

"I can be brilliant."

"And Capricorns," he said, pausing as if unsure of whether to continue.

"Tell me," I said. "Are they crazy?"

"No, no. Nothing like that," he said, smiling. "They tend to be *extremely* ticklish under their arms."

My eyes widened and my arms tightened close to my body, fearing Jeremiah would reach his hand toward my armpit, testing to see if I was ticklish. I imagined my loud squeal in the cathedral and its bursting echo bouncing off the walls. "We should go," I said urgently, but smiling.

I was really enjoying the dynamic we were developing. In so many ways he was unlike me, but we seemed to gel.

"You know," he said, "Capricorn is the astrological opposite of Cancer. So if you *are* a Capricorn, then we balance each other out."

Yes, I thought. *We do.*

DATE 24: WILL

Apparently, my television appearance yielded mixed reactions from virtual voyeurs. Most people were really supportive, and some even said they felt inspired to start their own dating projects. But the messages that stuck with me the most were the rude ones:

> Why would a guy want to go out with
> a woman he knows had 30 other dates
> in the last month? ech. do all women
> work like this? disgusting.

What in the world did he imagine I was doing with thirty guys? *Sleeping* with all of them? Was that really how he was defining a "date"?

I figured my critic was merely confused about my project. So I wrote back a long, poetic-sounding email that thanked him for his perspective and kindly explained the dates were extremely G-rated, that they were just *dates,* and that I was offering to pay for all of them. I even shared how my attitude was changing about men—how I actually found myself *loving* men—and how grateful I was for the thirty guys offering so much of their time for me.

His response?

Screw you and your spam, Tamara.

Mine:

Wow.
I just spent 20 minutes writing you.
Good luck.

The guy wrote me back again. And *that* time? His email was actually somewhat kind. Apologetic. He even admitted that he was a bit jealous of my receiving so much attention.

Why do boys have to be so confusing?!

The more time that went by, the more rude emails I received, mostly from guys commenting on my looks:

You're kind of cute but you have small tits.

Ouch!

I began to question my growing adoration for men. *Really, Tam?* I thought. *You think THAT guy could actually be "someone's Prince Charming"?*

I had spent three weeks immersed in a happy bubble, believing that men, in general, were wonderful. In just a few minutes, however, the crass notes from anonymous jerks seemed to unravel all my goodwill. The cynical, angry, "all men suck" side of me was in full force.

I could hear my mother's earnest tone looming in my head. *But Tamara, those mean comments have more to say about them than they do about you.*

Another negative comment popped up online:

> You are a sad individual. I read your
> blog and saw the TV segment. I almost
> feel sorry for you. But your problems,
> like most people's, are of your own
> making. Perhaps some good therapy or
> a spiritual connection will help you get
> over yourself. Narcissism should not
> be mistaken for high self-esteem. It is
> no wonder you are still single.

Rachel—always acting as my personal Tony Robbins—called me squealing with joy. "You've got haters! This is *fantastic.*"

"It *is?*" I said, momentarily distracted from my mental rampage against mean men.

"When you start getting haters, you've *made it.* Bring on the haters!"

Did I need to write back each of the haters? Defend my project? My love? My *boobs?*

And suddenly, I didn't need to worry about anything. Instead, my *dates* defended me. Proving that they were all modern-day "knights in shining armor," they drew their virtual swords and galloped to my defense.

First, a tidbit from Juan-Carlos, the handsome math teacher:

To the Negative Anonymous,

I find *you* to be a sad individual. You invoked narcissism in your principal critique, but have you given any thought as to why a private person such as Tamara would go to the trouble of bringing us this story? No, instead of looking for something positive, you quickly aligned yourself with some negative notion that she is sharing this with everyone in order to feed her own ego.

You do not know the first thing about Tamara: her background, her history, her personality, her sense of humor, her goals; you know none of these things. All you know are a few words that she has written plus a two minute video and you judge her based on that. Shame on you. Shame on you for judging anyone.

Sincerely,
Date 21

From Ryan, my Harlem miracle maker:

> I didn't get a chance to watch the TV
> segment, but I did go on a date with
> Tamara, so I will give my side: I think
> she is far from narcissistic. I feel like
> she is a woman who enjoys life to the
> fullest. She is a person that wants to
> enjoy living in the moment. The fact
> that she is single means she hasn't
> found the right one. I would rather be
> single than be with someone and real-
> ize they are not the one. I think ev-
> eryone is entitled to their opinion and
> thanks for sharing yours.

And finally, Billy, who took the ferry to the Statue of
Liberty and Ellis Island:

> Couldn't have agreed with Ryan more.
> Tamara was great on our date, and
> I am sure has been as well on every
> date she wrote about since day one . . .
> The guys who were the dates are
> also in the learning process . . . The
> dating scene for guys and gals can and
> should have the same amount of fun as
> she puts into it.

I was floored. Humbled. I figured *I* was the only one getting anything out of my project. But could some of the guys actually have gotten something out of spending just a few hours with me, too? And why in the world were they going out of their way to defend me?

♥

That night, I spent the evening hanging out with a guy who not only seemed to ignore negative criticism, but somehow welcomed it.

About a week before, I had received an email from Will, who I had met when I lived in Portland, Oregon. He was looking for a place in New York to crash for a couple nights and wondered if I could help him find a place. He was finishing his last semester in medical school and would check out the city's hospitals before deciding where he'd prefer to do his residency work. I made a deal with him: If he'd agree to be my date Saturday, he could crash on my couch for the two nights.

My idea went totally against my project's rules; I had required all my dates to be in a *public place.* So I rightfully justified my rule breaking: Will would be back in Portland on Valentine's Day, making him out of the running for a second date. Plus, I knew him well enough to feel comfortable with his sleeping in my living room. I had followed my own rules long enough that I finally knew when it was appropriate to break them.

He was a kind, fun, moral man who came from a good family. He was average height, with a round face and light blond hair, which looked stark white against his dark-framed glasses. He could play the piano and the organ like Mozart. And he had a theatrically flamboyant personality that made me wonder: Was he gay? British? Aiming to conduct a marching band? Or was he just unique and artsy?

After Will landed at JFK International Airport, we hurried to the Brooklyn Museum for its free-admission night. Instead of walking by the statues and paintings as normal art connoisseurs gazing silently at brilliance, Will suggested we put a spin on our journey.

"What if we take pictures of ourselves impersonating what we see?"

Next thing I knew, I was standing aside a statue of a Native American, clinging to a bow and arrow and imitating his warrior stance. Will kneeled beside the etched marble bust of a Neanderthal, squinted his eyes, and pursed his narrow brow. When we passed by exhibitions on furniture and home design, we played "which century is this piece of furniture from?" Everything appeared a little more vibrant with Will as my tour guide.

While we pretended to be art thieves dodging security guards, Will shared some stories about his life. He's the oldest of four children, did some missionary work in Argentina, and, although he's spent most of his time working hard and studying to be a doctor, has always found ways to fuel his creativity. Usually, he's most creative when he's around women.

I happen to like that in a man!

"Well," he said, looking down, "I did propose marriage last year."

"You *did*? To *whom???*" I beamed.

He rolled his eyes and looked me dead in the eye. "My sister."

"Wait. Wha—?" I said, with a soured look on my face.

"I know. It sounds gross. But I promise it wasn't like that."

"But you really did propose to your sister?" Was Will even nuttier than I thought?

"It's not bad. I promise," he said, waving his hands as if brushing away the suggestion. "Here's the thing. Every time my sister arrives at the airport in Portland, I try to give her a grand welcoming. You know how people bring flowers and signs saying WELCOME HOME! and all that?"

"Yeahhhh."

"Well, I always try to find ways to embarrass her. The first time she came to visit me, I got a bunch of friends together and held a thirty-five-foot banner for her that said, WELCOME HOME! LILY. She was *freaking out.*

"Of *course* the next time I had to outdo myself. So I borrowed a high school mascot uniform—one of those big ones with the horrible polyester outfit and the really big head. And her plane was delayed. That outfit was *so hot,* and I couldn't stop sweating in that thing. And remember—it's a *high school* uniform—so, like, thousands of kids have sweat in it. It smelled like gym class," he said, looking dramatically disgusted.

"So," I said, laughing, "how does all this lead to a marriage proposal?"

"Okay, yes," he said, composing himself. "So last year, she comes to visit, and I wasn't planning on doing anything. But she's like, 'What kind of embarrassing welcome do you have prepared for me this time?' So I *have* to do something, right?

"I go all out. Put on a tux with tails, buy two dozen roses and balloons, and make a big sign that says WILL YOU MARRY ME?"

"You didn't!" I yelled, turning to see if other museum goers had heard me.

"I did! But then there was a bit of an issue," he said, raising his finger as if making an important point. "What I hadn't thought of was that a guy walking around in a tux with two dozen roses tends to draw a *crowd*. So *all* these people were watching me. And I was getting nervous, thinking about how this would all turn out. But I had to commit to my role, right?

"Then the people start coming off the plane. And *they* all join the huge crowd around me, too, wanting to see who I'm waiting for. So there are, like, *hundreds* of people around me.

"I lean down and press play on my portable CD player—which of course is blasting that Celine Dion song from *Titanic*. And people seem to just keep gathering and gathering from everywhere. And my sister is at the *back* of the plane, so the entire plane of people is crowding around me.

"And then she comes out the gate and sees me. And she starts *laughing* and comes up to hug me. No big deal for her. She expected something crazy. But of course everyone *else* is *staring* at us. Totally silent."

"Oh, man," I said, "What did they *say?*"

"Well, that's the thing. Everyone around us is whispering to each other, 'What did she *say?*' 'Did she say *yes?*' and we just want to *leave*.

"But then it got totally awkward. One guy who'd been watching the whole time starts a chant, yelling, 'Kiss! Kiss! Kiss!'"

"They *didn't!*"

"They did!"

"What did you *do?*"

"Well. I mean, she's my little *sister*. So we look at each other and we're like, 'What do we do?' So I gave her a quick, authoritative, brotherly peck on the forehead—and we high-tailed it out of there, *right away*."

I giggled so much my cheeks hurt. Will lived life seeking the element of surprise. When we got back to my apartment, he announced an art activity he had planned.

"So," he said, digging into his carry-on luggage, "I could only bring as many little paint bottles as the TSA would let me, but—" He pulled out a sandwich bag filled with six small bottles of paint, along with a couple paintbrushes, a bottle of water, and some paper. He set it all on my kitchen table and established his instructions.

"Now, I already made a list of some things we need to paint," he said, pointing to a list with random items: a moon, a bridge, a trumpet, a white tuxedo, a book, a clock pointing to 2:00 AM. "Just pick which ones you want to draw, and I'll draw the others."

I had no idea why I was drawing them, but by that time, I figured Will would have some sort of outlandish ending to our project. I carefully painted the clock, the book, and the tuxedo, and he kept peeking at my work. "Am I doing this all right?" I asked.

"Oh, what you're doing is great! This is going perfectly." We cut out the pieces and laid them all out on a piece of paper.

He began to narrate.

"Tamara and Will are walking by the river near a bridge." He then grabbed his bottle of water, poured a bit into his hand, and started to flick water around. "Oh, and it's raining. Do you know where we are?"

"Portland?"

"Yes! Okay, so the moon is out," he said pointing at the moon and then the clock. "It's two in the morning, and there's a guy wearing a white tuxedo playing a trumpet outside the bookstore. We walk closer to the bridge, where there's a little black building and a long line outside. Do you know where we are now?"

"Voodoo Doughnuts?" I said, guessing the shop that had gained fame for quirky doughnut toppings like bacon and cereal.

"Yes!" he said proudly. He dug into his suitcase and pulled out a bag of donuts he had bought before catching his plane to New York. "I *had* to bring you a little bit of Portland."

I squealed and hugged him. "I can't believe you *did* that!"

I admired that he had gone out of his way to make the experience memorable and unique. And his wonderful ability to make a person feel special, like his sister, heedless of an entire airport of people ogling him, whispering, and potentially judging him, inspired me.

When it came right down to it, all the hate mail and detractors were meaningless. Let them laugh. Let them hate. Let them whisper. Let them *shout*.

I began this project because I wanted to learn something about men and dating, and I discovered so much more—about people in general, and myself. The one lesson that insisted on coming up again and again, however, was as simple as it was important: If you want love, give it away.

DATE 25: DAMON

While Will slept blissfully on my couch, I tiptoed out the front door at three in the morning for a full day's work, before heading out for my afternoon date. With just a handful of dates left before asking one of the thirty guys to be my thirty-first date, I felt mentally paralyzed. My inbox was filled with new requests for television and radio appearances, asking if I'd like to announce the big "winner" of my thirty-first date on air—and wondering if I would consider bringing my date on-air the next day.

Why do so many people care about my dating life all of a sudden? For years, my closest friends had been begging me to *stop* talking about the guys I was dating—or not dating. And now I felt that was all anyone wanted to hear about.

I had allowed myself to get so distracted by media appearances and by my growing crushes on some of the guys I'd already met that I had somehow let my most important assignment falter: getting more guys to go out with me. I had three empty slots for the remaining five days, including Monday, the next day.

How could I have fallen so behind on my planning? Throughout the whole project, I had managed to go into one date with at *least* the next date scheduled. Sometimes I even had dates scheduled for three or four days in advance. But even after getting some press and sending out "get me more guys" vibes to the universe, I was desperate for dudes. I started to lose my energy, feeling drained from dating every day.

I was tired of meeting new guys and feeling like I was on job interviews all the time, without any job offers. I wanted a break. I missed my girlfriends. I needed to *sleep*.

I was frustrated and preoccupied as I toured downtown with Damon. He was from Boston, another friend of Lumina's and apparently a handful of other mutual friends. He was obsessed with anything having to do with sound and music. He played guitar, wrote songs, and spent his money on concerts. Professionally, he specialized in recording and mixing voices, noises, films, and songs. Sound not only resonated through his soul; in some way, it defined him.

He was a tamer version of Jack Black, walking in zigzags with a devilish smile and a bounce in his step. He even looked like Jack, but with light brown hair and a cuter smile. Sometimes he'd whistle while spinning in a circle or jumping over a crack. He even clicked his heels in the air, and I swear it was higher than anyone I've ever seen on Broadway.

His carefree, energetic attitude was a good lift to my low energy. I tried bouncing along with him as we passed some famous landmarks: the U.S. Customs House, Federal Hall, the bronze bull near Wall Street. We walked by Ground Zero, which had changed over the years. While the hallowed ground remained quiet and respected, there was a new feeling of reverence mixed with hope. Visitors snapped pictures of the construction on the Freedom Tower. And children petted K-9 dogs who had become heroes while helping with the 9/11 search and rescue teams.

Just a few blocks away was the historic Trinity Church, with its tall, Gothic towers, stained-glass windows, and an organ that seemed to lure Damon into a trancelike state.

"That thing's *amazing*," he said, gazing in awe. "That's the Marshall & Ogletree."

"That's the what?" I asked, raising an eyebrow. *Is he seriously geeking out about a pipe organ? I love it.*

"I know, it looks just like any other organ. But it's actually not even a *real* pipe organ."

"It's not?" I stared at what appeared to look like any other organ I'd seen old ladies hovering over at church.

"The original organ was here forever, but it was damaged in the 9/11 attacks," he said, rubbing his chin, still gazing. "*This* one's only been here a few years. And it's all digital."

"Uh-huh," I said, looking more closely to see if I could see evidence of computers anywhere. I couldn't. It still looked like a regular, boring organ to me.

"The sound system on that thing is *amazing*. Like none other out there. It's got a tone-generation system. Totally software based. Basically, the company that made it dubbed the sounds of thirty other organs and then mixed them all together. Took them forever to get the sound just right. But the tone sounds even *better* than a real pipe organ. It's like a perfect tone, but it also gives those little imperfections in its sound so that it doesn't sound electronic.

"And it's *huge*. The computers alone literally weigh a *ton*." He rubbed his chin again, as if he were considering whether to run up to the organ and play it. "I know it must sound weird," he said, "but I've basically been obsessed with that instrument for *years*."

What was even weirder to me was that somehow I felt as if the silent presence of that instrument was teaching me something about my own metamorphosis. *Have I really spent so much time seeking lessons throughout the project that I'm now learning from some glorified synthesizer?*

Just as the church was forced to retire its original pipe organ, my old dating life had been so badly damaged that it had also needed to be carefully placed in the basement. And then there were the manufacturers who melded the sounds from thirty organs to create a new, remarkable tone. Maybe that's what my thirty-one dates would do for me and my own ability to love. Somehow, each of them would mix in my heart to create something unique and beautiful.

As we continued our self-guided tour, I noticed a little more energy in my walk. Even though I was tired and still lacked a booked calendar, I felt close to the end of the road and somehow knew that my long, arduous journey would be worth it.

Of course, the whole time I was jumping and skipping I was still in producer mode, debating how in the world I would track down a guy for the following day. So I headed from Trinity Church to another church—mine—and hoped to scope out some dates at a special evening service for single adults.

When I arrived at church, I noticed a significant change in the way it looked. The carpet was the same ivory color, the wooden pews were just as hard, and the lights seemed just as bright. But after spending weeks immersed in my own bubble of cute boys and living a life open to new ideas, I felt I was returning as a different person. It was like that feeling you get walking back through the halls of your old high school: I felt like I was looking at a familiar environment with a completely different set of eyes. Typically, I would have entered a room of single adults and scanned it, looking for any new, handsome faces. But this time, I just assessed myself. *Do I still fit in here? Have I actually changed? For the better?*

Just then a familiar shape weaved her way toward me, ready to spout her words of cynical wisdom. "After all the time you've been spending with guys, you show up here *without* a man for me?"

I hugged Rachel as if I hadn't seen her for months, holding on to her tightly, relishing the sudden dose of joy that overwhelmed me. I felt like I might cry. "You have no idea how great it is to see *girl*friends," I heaved.

No matter how much I had fallen in love with men over the last few weeks, there was no replacement for the gift of good girlfriends.

"Aw, poor you," she said playfully. "Life's so hard having to date every day."

"I know, I know—"

"No one's feeling sorry for you," she said, shaking her finger at me. "So what are you doing here, anyway? Aren't you supposed to be out on a date?"

"No, I went out with this guy Damon earlier today."

"Shut *up*," she said, squeezing my arm, desperate for details. "Damon? From *Boston?*"

"You know him?"

"Do I *know* him? I'm in *love* with him. And we'll get married someday—once he remembers he met me for two-point-five seconds. And then he'll realize I'm the only woman for him, and he'll ask me to bear his children."

"Oh, that sounds lovely," I said.

"I can't believe you went out with him. I hate you. So why are you here? Why aren't you writing or working or sleeping or whatever? Are you actually taking a break?"

"I'm scouting for dates."

"You still need some? How many?"

"Three more until my whole calendar's booked. My biggest problem is that I still have tomorrow night open. You wanna be my pimp?"

"Honey, I was born to be your pimp," she said, turning around to a boy sitting behind her. He looked like the kind of guy who belonged on one of those billboards for fancy colognes. He probably smelled nice, too.

"Hi, I'm Rachel," she said, to him. "And that's Tamara." She pointed my way and I gave him an amused but embarrassed smile. "How would you like to be her date tomorrow night for a dating project? It'll be fun."

He looked a little frightened of Rachel, slowly shrugging his shoulders. "Sure?"

"Fantastic," she said, turning back to me with authority. "Now, that wasn't so hard, was it? Let's get you those two more, and then you'll be done."

She whisked away just as I turned to lock eyes with the man who had wooed me with his mysterious Italian whispers. There was Adam, smiling widely with his perfect teeth framed by his unforgettable plump lips. As I gazed at him, I felt the intense rush of my crush for him. He had been the first to kick-off a long series of daydreams about men I had gone out with: Adam, then Evan, Jared, Allen, Christian, Tyler, Jonathan, Juan-Carlos, Derek. Were those crushes *real*? Or was I just swooning by circumstance?

"Tamara!" he said, rushing to hug me.

His vibrant energy captured me just as it had during our seemingly never-ending date. I felt as if I were being transposed back to my bubble of bliss. "Y'know," he said, smiling, "I was thinking of you the other day."

"You *were?*" Did he miss me? Want me?

"I was sitting down to watch TV, and I thought, *She is still going,*" he said through his infectious laugh. "I felt exhausted just *thinking* about how tired you must be."

"Yes," I laughed, "it's been tiring."

"What are you doing here?" he asked.

"Actually, I'm looking for dates."

"Are you kidding?" he laughed. "Okay, let me help."

My smile widened, and I realized my feelings for him *were* real. Seeing him again reminded me of all the laughter and smiles we had shared on that one simple date. If my crush for him felt validated so quickly, then certainly those feelings I had for the *other* men were real too. Weren't they?

Adam called his friend over. "Steve, this is Tamara. You know, the one doing the 31 Dates project?"

Just then, Rachel dragged over the cute, model-looking boy she had scared earlier—apparently named Dan—and another guy, named Tyson. I was surrounded by men waiting to hear me explain the requirements for dating me. It was a scene I could never have imagined for myself. In the past, I had watched gaggles of girls surround single men, each flipping her hair in desperate hopes of being noticed. Since when had I become the center of men's attention?

I briefly explained my project and mentioned that I was hoping to ask one of the thirty guys on a second date for Valentine's Day. Tyson was wide-eyed, intensely focused, like he was prepping for a competitive challenge.

"How will you be picking that guy?"

"I'm probably going to put a poll online to help narrow down the choices, and then I'll pick from there. And"—I hesitated on the next piece of information, hoping it wouldn't deter any of them from going out with me—"there's also a chance that the thirty-first date might be asked to join me on national television the next morning."

Adam's laughter broke through our circle. "Are you *serious*? You might go on television with this?"

Tyson looked absolutely delighted. Steve cowered. Dan still looked hot.

"Yeah," I said, "it sounds as if I'll definitely be going back on television for this. Of course, it'll be up to the thirty-first date whether he'd be comfortable with appearing on national television, too."

"You guys *have* to do it," Adam said, as if he were a sales-guy promoting a business product. His reaction made me think that Adam—while he was supportive and friendly—probably wasn't interested in me romantically. *Was he?* Then I realized that it didn't matter; my crush stood independent of whether he liked me in return, which seemed like a big change in the way I approached men. I always wanted cute boys to like me back. Who wouldn't?

But even if *none* of the guys liked me, I would still be okay. For the first time in a long time, I felt like my self-esteem wasn't dependent on whether a boy liked me back.

I allowed myself a mental celebration. I felt like I was making an emotional breakthrough. My calendar was officially *full*. The only major decision left to make was the ultimate one: Who would be Date 31?

DATE 26:
DAN

Even nasty bowling shoes couldn't detract from Dan's good looks. He was tall and muscular and had beautifully tanned skin and brown eyes. Even though he was good looking, I wasn't automatically in a swoon. I'd somehow become level-headed, had met plenty of good-looking guys who hadn't gelled with me, and was waiting to see if a crush would slowly develop, as it had with some of the other guys I'd gone out with.

We met at a bowling alley in Harlem that seemed to be hidden on the third floor of a random building. Even though it required elevator access, which was unlike any other bowling alley I'd been to, it had that familiar smell of sweat and recycled shoes, and it was just as big and busy as any other bowling alley in America. I grabbed my pair of rental shoes and barely had the chance to properly reintroduce myself to Dan before he blurted, "I'm twenty-one."

Time slowed while I took a split second to absorb what he'd just said.

"Is that a big deal for you?" I asked.

He stuttered his response. "N-no. I just thought you should know."

Had I met him just a few weeks before and learned he was ten years my junior, my mind would have screeched to a halt as little love warriors built a blockade around my heart. I would have spent the evening acting like his mentor or a big sister, instead of a new girl on a date. But surprisingly, I wasn't bothered that Dan was the youngest guy I'd ever gone out with. Mostly because I wasn't sure whether I was emotionally attracted to him. His announcement seemed premature.

But I was familiar with his approach. In the past, I would sometimes decide why a guy wouldn't like me and I would warn him of my off-putting qualities as quickly as possible. Like, "I don't drink," or, "I might be a Capricorn," or even, "I'm thirty-one." When Dan told me his age, it didn't make me think, *He's too young for me.* Instead I wondered, *Why is he telling me that I can't like him?* Who was he to decide for me?

I wanted to know all about him. What had he done in his twenty-one years? What were his hopes and dreams? I wanted to figure out what gave him the softness in his eyes and the solid confidence in his stature. I wanted to get to know who he was, regardless of his age.

"So, where do you live?" I asked. "I know nothing about you, other than the fact that my friend coerced you into going out with me."

"Jersey."

"You came from *Jersey* to go out? How long was your commute?"

"An hour or so," he said casually.

"An *hour?*" I was still amazed at how far some of the guys were willing to travel to be part of this project.

I dug my fingers into the holes of a pink eight-pound ball and felt its weight pull down my wrist. I walked to the bowling lane's line. I lowered the ball and gave it a gentle nudge and release. It crawled down the lane, slowly making it into the gutter.

I bit my lip, knowing I was about to suffer a great defeat.

When the mechanical gate reset all of my still-standing pins, Dan stepped up to the line and launched his bowling ball, and all the pins smacked down loudly at once.

That same scenario played itself out throughout the first game: Dan would knock most of his pins down after my ball pretty much guttered out, as if pulled by some magnetic force. *You can't win them all,* I reminded myself. If nothing else, the lack of competition allowed for some breathing room and time to learn about each other.

"Did you grow up in Jersey, too?" I asked.

"No, I'm from Arizona. Just out here for the Coast Guard. But I'm leaving in a couple months."

"Are you getting shipped out?"

"No, I mean I'm leaving the Coast Guard," he explained casually. "I just had a pacemaker put in, so I have to leave."

"You had a *what?*" Surely I hadn't heard him correctly. "Are you *okay?*"

"Yes, I'm okay. It's really not a big deal," he said.

"What happened?"

"Last summer, I was playing football and noticed some chest pains . . . a little fatigue. So they did all these tests. Turns out I get diagnosed with this thing called bradycardia. It just means I have a really low heart rate. So a few months later, doctors implanted a pacemaker to pick up my heart's rhythm." He wasn't bummed or scared or even fazed by it. He was just very matter of fact and accepting.

I stood still, sure my jaw was gaping. Somehow he thought our age difference would be tough for me to swallow. Ha! What was difficult was trying to understand how a twenty-year-old guy could require the same kind of surgery as a grandpa—and be so calm about it.

"Do you want to see it?" he asked.

I scrunched my nose and nodded. "I kinda do."

He pulled down the collar of his shirt just enough for me to see a small scar sitting on top of a bump the size of a Peppermint Pattie. Had he already dealt with the heavy thoughts of his mortality? Or was I just reacting the way a worried grown-up would?

"Your mother must have *freaked* out."

"Yeah," he said, "but this isn't something that requires daily maintenance. It's not like I'm *dying*. It's just a pacemaker. I can still do things. I just can't be in the Coast Guard anymore."

"So," I said, not really sure if I should treat him as a delicate patient or a tough military guy, "are you fully recovered? From the surgery and everything?"

"Finally. It took a couple months. Actually," he said, moving his arm, "I wasn't allowed to lift my left arm until just a few weeks ago."

"Should you be *bowling?* We can stop. It's not like I'm even close to beating your nonstop strikes and spares."

"I'm all right," he assured me, grabbing the ball and walking to the line again. "I can even play football."

"So," I uttered, still concerned about his heart but trying not to make a big deal about it. I was starting to feel like his concerned big sister. "Do you play football a lot?"

"Are you kidding? Not playing football was the hardest part of my recovery. That's, like, my *life*. I would kill to just play it every day of my life."

"So then what do you want to do after you leave the Coast Guard?"

"What do I *want* to do? Or what am I *gonna* do?" he said as the ball crashed into the pins again.

"Does there have to be a difference?"

"I *want* to go to college and play football, but I just don't see that happening."

"Because of your pacemaker?"

"No. Because I'm not sure I can get onto the team. I want to go to BYU. But even if I get into the school, the football team is *really* competitive."

My thoughts turned away from Dan's heart and reflected on my own heartbreak. I had known someone who had played football for BYU. He had dumped me while we were riding on the subway just a few months before. And hadn't spoken to me since.

"I know someone who played there. He might be willing to talk to you about how tough the competition really is." Could I really communicate with Mr. Beautiful But Boring once again? I imagined the email correspondence.

"Dear BBB,

Remember how you dumped me and I
felt like I was the biggest dating disaster in the world so I produced a project

to figure out what was wrong with me when it came to dating and dealing with all men who were in my presence?

No? Anyway, I met this one guy . . . "

Maybe putting Dan in touch with my ex wasn't the best idea.

"Are you at least gonna try to apply?" I asked.

"I'm not sure. I kind of don't see the point."

And that's when I found myself turn from girl-on-a-date to woman-with-ten-years-more-experience. He was young, but I felt as if I could see a big future ahead of him. Lots of potential. "Dan, if you don't ask, the answer's always no. You have to at least try."

"I guess."

"I just believe that most obstacles in our lives are not other people or things or events. Usually the biggest challenge is that we're standing in our own way of what we want. We limit *ourselves*. And then obstacles present themselves to show us how much we really want something. They help us decide if we're willing to push further to get what we want."

"You really believe that?"

"I *have* to believe that. That belief is the only reason I've made it this far in anything in my life. It's the only reason I'm still doing this project. And it's the only reason I have a date tonight. When you get out of your own way, that's when you start to see miracles happen. Am I making sense?"

"Yeah, I get what you're saying."

"I mean—what if your issues with your heart and everything are just giving you a new opportunity to go after what you *really* want?" I asked, walking up to the line to take my turn. I'm not sure if it was a case of strong focus on my part or sheer luck, but somehow my ball stayed in the middle of the lane, knocking down all ten pins in its path.

"I just made a strike!" I yelled in shock.

Dan gave me a high five. "I knew you could do it!"

"See, Dan? Miracles *do* happen," I said, laughing.

And they really do. I needed the reminder. Dan's attitude about his pacemaker was exactly what I needed. He helped me realize that a broken heart doesn't have to be the end.

So what did I *really want?* Had my hopes changed?

I had launched my dating project hoping to learn something about men and wanting to recover from being the world's worst dater. But my priorities had seemed to shift as I had unexpectedly started falling for some of the guys. What would happen after I ended the project? Anything?

If nothing else, I knew I would finish the project with at least one second date, and it was my job to figure out who would be the right fit. When I got home that night, I sent out an email to every guy I'd gone out with and outlined my steps to determining who would be Date 31.

Hey guys,

My plans for Valentine's Day seem
to be a bigger extravaganza than I'd

originally planned, so let me know if you're even interested.

After Date 30 on Friday, I'll post an online poll listing the names of every guy who's willing to be my 31st date. The results will serve as two-thirds of the decision. My preference makes up the remaining one-third of the vote. So let me know if you're up for being part of the "man poll."

I've been asked to be on a couple morning shows and will announce the name of the chosen guy on air around 8 AM. One of the shows might even want to call the guy on the phone.

So this will literally be like a "Can I have the envelope please" situation. I probably won't even know who it is until the show on Saturday morning, so it will be extremely short notice for you if you're chosen.

THEN. The date.

So far, I'm trying to nail down dinner plans for eight o'clock, but there might end up being some other stuff too. This date is, again, my treat.

Sunday morning, I have been asked to consider coming back onto at least one of the morning shows and maybe bring the chosen gentleman as well.

I realize that this is WAY MORE than your second dates might usually call for. I promise, I will not be insulted if you don't want to be part of it.

And who knows, maybe by now you have found another cute girl to take out on Saturday! If so, I want details!

-Tam

DATE 27: NICK

From the moment I first saw Nick, I knew I'd like him. He was slouching on a bench along the East River, gazing intensely into a copy of *The New Yorker* as if he were uncovering his own purpose in its pages. I slowed my pace upon my approach, staring at him and trying to figure him out. He appeared smart, handsome, and unassuming; I'd soon discover he was witty and laid-back, too.

"Nick?" I asked, wary of interrupting his reading. He lifted his eyes to me and smiled, appearing even more striking than I'd expected. He looked like a celebrity in disguise, parading the streets purposely unkempt. His hazel eyes matched the wisps of light amber hair poking from beneath a wool beanie with the word OBAMA proudly stitched above his brow. Nick's smile was like everything else, charming without appearing too perfect.

"What are you reading about?" I asked.

"The inauguration."

"I'm guessing you're a fan," I said, pointing to his hat.

He looked upward, as if reading the presidential embroidery. "I am. I was just down in D.C. for the inauguration, blogging about it, actually," he said, stuffing his magazine into a messenger bag.

"Who do you write for?"

"Officially? Not really anyone. Unofficially? A lot of people."

We walked up a set of stairs that led to the city's tram, which looked like a big gondola above the East River. We were taking it to the nearby two-mile-long Roosevelt Island.

"How was the inauguration?" I asked.

"Supremely *awesome*," he said, with undeniable pride and righteousness.

We reached Roosevelt Island in just a few minutes, but it seemed a world away. It had a totally different feel from Manhattan—it was tiny, with few people, and rows of tall buildings hovered over barren streets. I wondered if anyone even lived there, and compared with New York City—heck, compared with *any* city—few people do. The island is only about two miles long, with one main road, a sidewalk that stretches around the island's perimeter, and the basic stores for its residents: a small grocery store, a barber shop, a school. It was a stark contrast with neighboring Manhattan.

Nick narrated our journey across the island with stories from the inauguration, describing the president's new cabinet with fluffy sentences that sounded something like, "providing the necessary vicissitude needed to resolve the apathy and ennui so prevalent in the overly antiquated autocratic regime."

He would interrupt his own stories to point out a "horrifyingly wonderful" dilapidated building surrounded by an old, rusty fence. "That place is like a postapocalyptic world, just waiting for zombies to evacuate."

He spoke like few people I knew, lacing his words with pretentious vocabulary and linking thoughts in overly complex ways. With every sentence, I found myself feeling mystified, uncertain of who he was but increasingly fascinated. He read everything: nonfiction, literature, essays. He was a philosopher, a pundit, a storyteller, and an artist, and I was his audience.

He was often evasive, leading me to connect the dots. Like when he was telling me where he had lived: "D.C., Austria, Colorado, and New Haven."

His geographic blend seemed a strange mix. "New Haven? Why'd you live there?"

He looked away with intended humility. "School."

Why couldn't he just say, "I went to Yale"?

He majored in political science and still kept up with politics.

"I work on campaigns every couple years," he said. "Last fall I toured the country while blogging for the Rock the Vote campaign."

"Do you want to be a politician?"

"Oh, *no*," he said, looking aghast. "I'm an actor. I've just been around politics forever. My family is *very* political," he said with a weighted tone, as if he were intentionally hiding his pedigree. I imagined his parents to be famous politicians or activists who greatly influenced his education and opinions.

His passions were vast, and he was a mishmash of contradictions. He had the wit and flair of Jon Stewart and the depth and artistry of Vincent van Gogh. His passion for politics and activism, paired with his verbosity, made him the model of a perfect political candidate. But he seemed to deviate from his prep-school brilliance by donning T-shirts and ripped jeans, which made him look more like a pothead frat boy than a bureaucrat in the making. And he would make silly expressions, contorting his face to appear unhandsome-ish.

Why do I feel as if he's trying to act like someone he's not?

Still, his depth and defiance were intoxicating. With every comment or quip, I found myself swept away into his stories. He was confusing and intimidating—and I loved it. The more he talked, the more powerful a spell he cast over me.

"Let's go check out the view from there," he said, pointing to the tallest building on the island. We walked to the front office, where Nick requested a tour. "We'd like to check out an apartment."

The woman at the desk handed him a clipboard with a pen and piece of paper. "Fill this out and I can take you up."

Nick spent several minutes filling out the form. "What should my name be?" he asked. "Dr. Fisher McSimmons?"

"Sure," I said. "Are you really lying to get up and look at an apartment?"

"If that's the only way to get up to the top of the building, then who cares? Besides, what's fun without some scurious shenanigans? What should your name be?" he asked, setting his pen on the empty line for "spouse."

"Uh . . ." *Does he really want us to pretend we're married?* "Whatever name you want," I said.

"You can be Felicia." And just like that, he wrapped me into his world of make-believe.

He was the perfect mix of mirth and mischief, filling out every line meticulously with fake email addresses, emergency contact information, and references. The woman at the counter glanced at the paper and set it aside. "Are you looking for a one- or two-bedroom?"

"That depends," he said. "We're really hoping to find something with a great view."

She grabbed a heavy set of keys and walked toward the elevator. "I've got just the right place."

We made our way to a one-bedroom apartment on the twenty-first floor, where there was an amazing view from the balcony. Across the river was my city, looking strong and intimidating with its skyline of towering buildings. I turned to the woman. "How different is it living here than in the city?"

"Oh, *this* is still New York City," she insisted.

I looked back across the river, comparing the difference in the two islands. Roosevelt Island might technically be in the same county as Manhattan, but there was no comparison. I felt as if I were somehow the Jiminy Cricket of the crew, wanting to announce the truth to the people around me, desperately shouting in a tiny voice, "This is *not* New York City!" and, "Nick, you're way more amazing than you're letting on!"

On our way back downstairs, Nick concocted a story about how we were also looking at loft apartments in SoHo while I watched him in wonder. Maybe Nick was just desperately trying to appear unspecial, which seemed impossible. Or maybe he was just doing his best to balance his smarts with his free spirit.

He reminded me of the artist-type boyfriends I adored in college who drew out my inner hippie. One had dreadlocks and a wiry beard and dreamed of living in a tepee. He had passion, creativity, and blue eyes the color of a tranquil ocean. My heart wanted so badly to follow him to live under the stars, but my mind loved the idea of sleeping in an apartment with running water too much.

Nick was a man who was still holding on to his tepee-type dreams, balancing his acting career with his passions for politics and storytelling. How could I judge such ambition? Somewhere between Zombieville and the tram, I fell for him even more. I stopped analyzing him and stopped wondering if I were smart enough. I just wanted to kiss him.

I imagined him pulling me close, looking into my eyes with shared determination, and kissing me passionately. I felt pure lust drumming its way through my bloodstream.

How was it that I had wanted him so badly so suddenly? My heart was swirling so much that I was ignoring the rationale in my head. Would I fall into an old habit of allowing my passion to control my body? Was what I felt with Nick real? If I kissed him, could it grow into a glorious love affair?

I knew in my most sane, centered self that lust doesn't last.

After all, passion is just one part. Eventually, pragmatism would weasel its way into all of my dating scenarios. Even my shaggy tepee lover from college ended up shaving and working on Wall Street.

Nick and I headed to the subway station to part ways. "I'll be out of town this weekend," he said, "so let me know who you end up going out with for your big thirty-first date."

I wanted so badly for him to reach out and kiss me in desperation. Instead, he gave me a parting hug, not holding me nearly long enough. I could feel my heart pounding in anticipation, wondering when I would see him next.

"Let's get together soon," he said. "Maybe next week we can meet up for coffee?"

"That'd be great," I said, but I sensed his disinterest, and my disappointment set in when I realized he was just drawing me into another story.

I went home and whimpered, feeling unraveled. *How did I end up liking so many of these guys?*

I called Rachel. "Am I stupid?"

"What kind of crazy nonsense are you talking about now?"

"I just feel like this project is the dumbest thing I've ever done."

"Are you kidding? Then it's the most brilliant dumb thing ever," she said.

"I feel like I'm spending all this time with these great guys, only to realize in the end that I'll end up lonely forever. Is that lame?"

"Oh, honey. That's so normal it's ridiculous. You're just overwhelmed."

"That's true."

"Was your date okay today?" she asked.

"Yeah, it was fine."

"And what about that guy Dan? How was bowling?"

"Fine. He's twenty-one."

"Oh, crap—"

"It was no problem, seriously," I said.

"I'm sorry I pimped you out to a fetus."

"It really was okay," I said. "I'm just wondering if all this was worth everything I put into it."

"Forget the guys for a second. Have you learned anything through all this?"

"Yes. A *lot*."

"Okay, like what?" she probed.

I thought for a second before answering, remembering the many lessons each date had taught me. "That it's important to take a risk. That guys don't all suck. That my broken heart was actually worth it. And that even if I do end up alone forever, it's really gonna be okay."

"Honey, you're already way more than okay."

DATE 28: TYSON

By the next day, I'd recovered from my mini-breakdown and spent my energy preparing a short television segment on Valentine's Day recipes. Elena tapped on the door and walked in, looking like she had something important to discuss. "So," she said, sitting in the comfy chair next to my desk, "what are you going to do with all the leftovers?"

"The *what?*"

"Leftovers. The guys you *don't* pick for Valentine's Day."

"It's not like I'm getting married," I said.

"I know, but . . . "

"So hopefully I'll go out on second dates with some of the other guys another time. But it's not like I'll end up dating a bunch of them or anything."

"Right. So what about the *other* ones?" she asked, leaning closer to me.

"Elena," I said, realizing she wasn't really asking about *my* future dating prospects, "are you asking about a certain guy in particular you'd like to meet?"

Her disposition brightened. "Maybe."

By that time, most girls I knew had picked a favorite. Ryan was adored for the heart he'd shown in Harlem. Some girls wanted Jason to teach them to tango. Others liked Collin's quirkiness, saying they wanted to date him *and* Zantar. And Juan-Carlos seemed to have the adoration of every woman—including my mother. Every date had his own unorganized, anonymous fan club. I was the only one who had trouble narrowing my list for a potential Valentine's Day date, and the competition was getting tough.

I spent the evening with Tyson, who'd appeared eager about my project ever since I had met him at church on Sunday. He thought like a fellow producer, suggesting several date ideas, and thoroughly investigated each option. We settled on meeting for authentic Chinese dumplings, but there were so many good places, we couldn't decide. His idea? He mapped out a route to the most highly touted dives in Chinatown, each offering huge helpings of dumplings for about $2. It was like a treasure hunt. It was a blast.

One of the things that was so much fun about this project was that it forced me (and the guys) to get creative about dates. I'd never had so much fun exploring New York, and it reminded me that thinking outside the box could yield not only new experiences and insights, but great people as well.

Tyson and I consulted our map and set our course. Each spot had its own unique draw. There was the dark hole-in-the-wall where people squished their way inside for Styrofoam containers filled with cheap, salty, tasty dumplings, then the sterile shop with the overwhelming smell of Chinese takeout where the woman behind the counter barked orders, demanding we choose quickly and correctly. "You order six at a time. No more." There was the clean, hip joint that played soft-rock music and had bland, doughy dumplings that required lots of sauces. But my favorite was our last stop, a busy restaurant that offered relatively fine dining at low prices. This was where Tyson and I finally sat down to eat while I rested my aching feet.

We'd been so busy running from one spot to the next, I hadn't really taken a good look at him. Tyson looks like he could be the lead singer of an indie-rock band, with his cool, ironically disheveled blond hair, piercing blue eyes, and smile that could make girls want to follow him everywhere.

We were about halfway through our dumpling run when I realized our brisk trek was analogous to Tyson's life, whisking from one adventurous spot to the next. He loves traveling so much that he even became a flight attendant—just one of his many jobs—so he could see the world for free.

As he ticked off all the countries he'd visited, I counted them on my fingers: China, India, Trinidad, Brazil, Israel, Nicaragua. I ran out of fingers pretty quickly. In all, he rattled off thirty-six countries. That's a lot of countries to see by the age of thirty-one.

"And I'm planning on heading to Ecuador this spring," he added.

I was swept into his stories, as he told me about tackling the riskiest adventures. He swam with stingrays. He went skydiving and quickly saved his own life after his foot was caught in the line to his parachute. Most recently, he had challenged the bulls in Costa Rica.

What drove this wanderlust? I wondered. Could one have romantic wanderlust as well?

I consider myself a pretty curious woman—no surprise there—but his curiosity seemed downright insatiable. Not only did Tyson have a lot of interests, he was also *interesting*. He had just moved to the city from his home in Vancouver, British Columbia, on a whim. He was a documentary filmmaker who had created his own production company and was in the midst of applying to graduate school for documentary studies. He enjoyed writing, had already published two books, and was working on his third. And while he juggled his life as a flight attendant/author/filmmaker/hopeful grad student, he also dabbled in selling real estate. Tyson was the ultimate Renaissance man. Quite frankly, he was more than the kind of man I dreamed of dating—he was the kind of person I wanted to *be*.

He was charming, successful, entrepreneurial. He even had *skills* I coveted. He spoke Spanish, played several instruments, loved to sail. And he used pretty words, like "pescatarian" (which he used to describe me) and "dizygotic" (which he used to describe himself).

"Most people just say 'fraternal twins,'" I said.

As he continued listing his accolades and avocations, my mind drifted into the future, wondering what life would be like if Tyson and I were to realistically date after my project. Usually those imaginary journeys seem romantic and sepia-toned, with shaded edging. Sometimes they're in slow motion.

I would be my most perfect self, holding hands with my handsome suitor as we ran away with the wind whipping through my perfectly untangled hair. Sure, I was fantasizing the backdrop of a cheesy tampon commercial, but hey, that's what daydreaming's all about.

But with Tyson, my imagination drifted somewhere a little different. I fast-forwarded a few months down the road. We would discuss dreams, hobbies, work with equally heightened energy. We would become Mr. and Mrs. Über-Couple, conquering the world one overly obsessive adventure at a time.

And then, with just as much passion, we would argue, as if our love for our personal interests would compete with our feelings for each other. He would grow resentful of my unpredictable work schedule. I would hate how he traveled so often with little warning. Our arguments would escalate until eventually I would clench every part of my body tight until I was forced to release the pressure. I would then unleash my attack, screaming like a wild woman, filled with rage and resentment.

"Vegetable dumpling?" interrupted a whispery voice.

I shook my head and looked up at the server, who smiled at me. Had Tyson seen my eyes cloud over? Had my expression changed to reveal my darker thoughts?

"Yes, that's mine," I said, forcing a smile in return.

My instant flashes of foresight threw me off guard. I didn't even know Tyson, and already I was predicting a passion-filled breakup.

Maybe I was just projecting warning signs because of what I had experienced with some men I'd dated in the past. At first glance, we would boast "We have a strong connection," but our similarities and those very same commonalities would become the root of our battles. Discussions once based on passion and love would turn to anger and jealousy.

Just as my cabbage-and-carrot-filled dumpling needed a little soy to bring out its natural sweetness, I needed someone to add just a touch of zest to my life without competing with it. I wanted the sweet *and* the sour, not just an overload of one.

Maybe Tyson and I are just the same flavor.

In talking to him, it was clear we were equally neurotic about living full, "productive" lives that were passionate and lively. The more we talked, the more I saw our similarities. And it drove me crazy.

I decided in the middle of my second-to last bite that despite how handsome, accomplished, and creative he was, it would never work. I have to admit that I was a little relieved. I had enough men on my plate already, and—like the myriad dumpling houses we'd visited today—each guy had his own allure, his own exceptional quality that drew me to him. Choosing the best on the block would be no easy feat.

DATE 29:
PAUL

With just a few more days to go, I finally felt like the whole project was coming together. I had sacrificed sleep and (as odd as it sounds) my social life to completely immerse myself in a world of men and first dates, and for the first time I could see the finish line.

In the meantime, I needed to plan my second-date extravaganza for Valentine's Day. I called around to find a fancy restaurant that wouldn't mind hosting me, my date, and the *Good Morning America* camera crew that I'd already agreed could come along for dinner. I also needed to track down some theater tickets, which seemed to be a bit of a challenge. A lot of the guys had gotten back to me, saying they'd be up for a second date, knowing it would be a circus.

Others had opted out, saying they'd be out of town or, like Brian, the forty-year-old online dating pro, they'd already met someone new. And then there were guys like Jared, my ice-skating Minnesota man. He sent me a sweet email saying he'd love to join me on Saturday night if he ended up being picked, followed by this:

> P.S. To be completely honest, I would have a great time, but if you think you may have found your true Prince Charming and have met the one guy that you're hoping wins at the polls, leave me out of the equation and raise the chances that you'll get him.

Today was Thursday. Tomorrow afternoon, I would list the names of potential thirty-first dates online that would count for two-thirds of the vote. Right away, campaigns started popping up all over the Internet. Friends of mine had created Facebook fan pages for their buddies—titled Vote for Joel or Peter for #31!—and spammed every person they'd known since grade school, looking for voters.

Evan's sister completely revamped her own website, turning it into official headquarters for the Campaign for Evan, complete with pictures and explanations for why he should get the votes. "He loves kids!" she wrote, followed by a video testimony from his nieces and nephews talking about how much they loved their uncle. "He has skills!" which was followed by pictures of him cooking, surfing, sailing, and potty-training her children. And finally, "He's musical!" depicted him playing the guitar and a shot of him in his high school band uniform. The competition between the guys and their various fan clubs was fierce.

I was excited and nervous for my last first date, whomever it would be with. I was already looking forward to a second date, but I still needed to stay focused on the dates remaining.

Paul was easy to spot among the crowd lingering outside Carnegie Hall, antsy for a night of classical music. After all, he was the only guy younger than seventy, not to mention he was on crutches.

When I'd met him briefly the previous fall, he had mentioned needing foot surgery because of an old running injury. I don't know what stood out more, his big smile or the gigantic white plaster cast that encased the lower half of his leg.

He hobbled along side me as we made our way into the theater. "It's hard to have a suave swagger on crutches," he said.

Paul had finagled some tickets with his student discount, while everyone else in the audience had probably used their senior citizens' deal. Our seats were about fifty feet from the stage, giving us a clear shot of the grand piano sitting alone on it.

The tiny woman sitting by me grabbed my arm lightly, smiling widely enough to show off her bridge peeking past her gums, and said warmly, "It's so nice to see young people here."

I pointed to Paul. "It's also nice to have a music mastermind guiding you through all the music." He had studied music at Dartmouth, before coming to New York to pursue his PhD in music history from Columbia University. He was in the midst of his dissertation on Franz Liszt, who's among the less noticed of the classical composers but equally as smart and influential.

"So, why are you spending so much time studying Liszt?" I asked.

"I know he's not as popular as Beethoven or anything, but he made a huge impact on classical music. He practically revolutionized the way music was played."

"How so?"

"He was a lot like a poet at the piano. He showed a huge range of emotion in his work—incomparable to any of his contemporaries. He was gutsy. He was kinda like the rock star of his time."

"An 1840s rock star?" I imagined a guy wearing a powdered wig and pleather pants, jamming on an electric guitar.

"Kind of! He was known as quite the ladies' man too," Paul said.

An 1840s rocker with groupies in corsets. Awesome.

As the music began, Paul relaxed into his seat like he was going into a meditative trance. He gave a slight nod every now and then, as if he were approving the players' execution. Was he analyzing every stanza? Or thinking of how he would play it differently?

Most of the music being played that night was written by Chopin. To me, Chopin was just a fancy old French dude who probably played for a king somewhere. I had heard some of his music before, but I would never have been able to identify his work the way I could spot songs by Madonna or Michael Jackson. For Paul, the music coming from the piano was just as familiar. He smiled and moved his head slightly, anticipating every shift in the notes. As he lost himself in the music, I stole glances his way. He was wholesome looking, with wispy blond hair and a distinct, handsome profile. He looked younger than he was but seemed to have an old soul, slowly nodding with the beat of the music.

During intermission, I assumed Paul would rush to express all his favorite highlights. Instead, he asked what I thought. "Do you like it so far?"

"I do," I said, "but I keep wondering what you've been thinking this whole time. Tell me about Chopin."

"He's pretty languid, isn't he?" he asked, as if there were no difference between Chopin's music and the man himself. "He was in love with a famous writer who ended up breaking his heart. In fact, Lizst introduced the two of them."

"Chopin and the writer girl?"

"Yep. They were together for a long time. You can hear their romance in his music, with all the soft, rolling tones," he said. I hadn't really noticed. Clearly, I had not listened to the song the same way he had.

"How's your project been so far? I've been dying to ask." Apparently, he was just as eager to hear about my field of study as I was to learn about his.

I told him how I worried that I wouldn't get my calendar filled, how I almost had to scope out guys at the coffee shop and beg them to fill spots, of my emotional breakdowns; I talked about my moments of insecurity and how I felt like I was overcoming them, and how really, this experience had been one of the best in my entire life.

I felt fully present with Paul, unafraid of showing my whole self. And it wasn't just because he was easy to talk to, but also because this entire monthlong process had helped me shed my fears about first dates. I could be honest and real and not distracted by constant inner self-criticisms or thoughts of whether the guy would like me or not.

The piano player returned to the stage and took his seat. Paul leaned over to whisper to me. "This next song might be . . . a little weird," he said with delightful warning.

It wasn't weird at all. It was just intense, with loud cymbals clashing and dissonant chords. The notes might not have sounded as if they were naturally expected to go together, but when they were paired, their opposition wasn't discordant. Instead, it was beautiful. Unexpected. I couldn't help but correlate the sounds to dating (of course), where two people might appear unmatched, but in reality, they fit perfectly, accentuating each other's uniqueness.

When the performance ended, we waited until everyone filtered out before heading to the exit.

Paul struggled to stand and winced, holding back a surge of pain with a silent gasp.

"Are you okay?" I asked, trying to help him.

"Doing great," he said, forcing his tensed jaw into a smile. Despite having had major surgery that apparently hadn't gone so well, he was putting on his best first-date performance, being kind and acting fully present.

Of course, I could relate. I had just spent a month showing each one of my dates my most positive self, in spite of my handicaps: little sleep, tough workday, bad attitude.

My quick analysis of Paul's classic first-date behavior had me wondering . . . had first dates become my own Liszt?

Paul immersed himself in studying a dead composer who few average citizens knew or cared about, because he saw Liszt's music as the foundation for so much of what everyone listened to in our day. And I had immersed myself in my own grueling field of study so that I could have a better foundation for dating.

Just as Paul dissected and analyzed music, I did the same with dating. He thought about movement and rhythm, while I thought about intentions and behavior. I was no longer just a girl moping around, hoping to get first dates right. In just a month's time, I had gone from a guaranteed relationship disaster to a woman with confidence in herself and men.

There was no way I could ever look at dating the same way again.

DATE 30: STEVE

A month before all of this, first dates felt a lot like getting hazed while rushing a college sorority: You can't help but wonder if you're being true to yourself as you willingly participate in sometimes humiliating circumstances that make you feel uncomfortably vulnerable. Some of my past first dates have been so painful that I would have preferred having my hair flushed down the toilet or walking blindfolded in my underwear through a graveyard at midnight. There was the prom date who spent the entire evening telling me about his crush on my best friend, the night I had my purse stolen from under my chair, the time I locked myself out and my date and I crawled through my bedroom window, and the night in college I found myself interrupting a guy professing his love for me as I threw up in his shoe.

My endurance through bad dates has earned me a rightful badge of honor, bonding me into a sisterhood of first-date haters, a sorority in which all of us wish we could avoid membership. Who in her right mind would put herself through all that again—thirty times over?

After my month of self-inflicted initiations, I had *finally* made it to graduation day. Yay! I had become a different dater altogether. The more guys I met, the more fun I had. I entered my project a cynic, thinking there were no good guys in New York, let alone any I would want to date seriously. And then, a mere month later, I found myself having mini-crushes on one too many, dreaming of second dates with at least a third of them, and considering each guy, at the very least, a friend I genuinely respected. Those changes alone seemed like a bigger miracle to me than Moses parting the Red Sea.

My change in attitude was constant but incremental, so I didn't notice it easily. Kind of like when I've lost weight and can't really tell until someone I haven't seen in a while points it out to me. Every so often, I noticed hints of slight evolution during unexpected moments. Like the day I sat on the subway and looked at all the people immersed in their own little worlds. A mother spoke quietly to a toddler who wouldn't sit still. And a weary-eyed man sporting a dirty uniform slouched into the seat across from me, likely resting from another predictable day at work before heading home to a noisy family. We all appeared so separate, even though we sat so close to one another.

And then a strange thought popped in my head. How would our dynamic change if there were some kind of emergency? Like a train crash, or a small fire, or any number of unexpected crises that would force us to acknowledge one another.

I imagined the sleepy man, while worried about his own destiny, would rally up as the leader, checking if everyone was okay. We'd be especially attentive to the mom and her child to make sure they felt safe. We'd work as a team to get away from the danger and home to loved ones. Strangers would become heroes.

In that little moment of imagined community, I felt healed. From what, exactly, I'm not so sure. But I could feel my soul stringing itself to everyone else around me as I wondered, *What if every stranger has some kind of hero hiding inside them?*

From that second, I realized that these men—these thirty guys who'd signed up for a dating game with some stringy-haired chronic ex-girlfriend—had not only changed the way I looked at dating, but also impacted the way I judged people.

I suppose it just happened at some point while I tried my best to see those guys as their true selves and remove all judgment about their wardrobes, their moods, their money, their emotional availability, and our potential compatibility. I finally understand the purpose of dating: not to learn *whom* to love, but to learn *how* to love.

I awoke the morning of my last first date with more energy than I'd had all month. I was more bouncy than usual during the date, asking Steve all about himself with a heightened happiness. I wanted to know everything: where he was from, how long he had been here, if he liked the city, his roommates, his job, his neighbors, his Laundromat—whatever. I was on full tilt. When I wasn't pelting him with questions, I was talking about everything around me: the barren baseball field that welcomed our arrival to Staten Island, the wind that kept smacking my face, and the dearth of restaurants and sites near the ferry terminal. I was downright manic.

Steve, for his part, seemed intimidated by me. He stood apart from me with shoulders squared, answered in brief sentences, and constantly diverted his eyes from mine. Maybe I overwhelmed him a little. Maybe he had just felt a little pressured into going out with me. Whatever it was, his body language said he was uncomfortable—even uninterested.

Got it.

I made a mental note to pipe down and give him more personal space as we walked into the Staten Island Museum, basically an old Victorian home converted into a small showcase of the borough's history, which was mostly old maps and stuffed birds.

Steve—a handsome, skinny, clean-cut guy with a magnetic smile—started opening up as we wound our way through the antiquated house. I'm sure it helped that I toned down my energy to a less frenetic level. Whatever the case, his shoulders relaxed and he seemed more at ease. He finally began answering my probing questions about his life. He had moved to New York for postdoctoral work in biochemistry. He spends long days and nights working in a lab. Instead of hanging out with people on weekend evenings, he often spends that time gazing into microscopes, trying to identify specific structures and patterns in human cells. Suffice to say, he isn't an extrovert like me. I must have been like a tsunami to his calm shore at the start of the date—no wonder he'd battened down the hatches. Understanding that helped me slip into my calmer demeanor—call it my sea breeze mode.

He went on to explain how he hopes the cells he's studying will someday reveal a big secret about the mysteries of humans. I admire smart guys, even find them attractive, but I wondered at the irony of his spending so much time trying to learn about humans without having much actual companionship.

"Sounds like we both want to know more about the way people function," I said.

He smiled, as if surprised that he and I would have something in common. "I guess we do," he nodded.

It's not that I was reaching for a connection, but I recognized it as a default pattern of mine during a first date—find the commonalities and the differences, and forge ahead. Steve was a smart guy—cute and nice, too—but at the moment, I felt a bit like I was keeping a distant cousin whom I'd just met company. There just wasn't a spark. And I couldn't help but think of the guys I had genuine connections with, wondering who would accompany me tomorrow. Still, I focused my attention on Steve, and on making the most of this last date.

Steve continued explaining his work, which I found genuinely interesting. Most of the time, his work is, to the untrained eye, pretty monotonous. But then every few months, Steve says, he notices something different on one of his slides. A tiny movement will reveal something big, giving him a new detour in his research.

"Yep," I said, "I can totally understand that. The little things? Making the biggest difference in what you've been finding? Same."

But just when I was beginning to think he spent his days alone in a dark lab, wearing clunky goggles and staring into cells, he blindsided me with a little nugget of information that sort of threw me for a loop. He surfs.

"In fact," he added, "I've surfed with one of the guys you went out with. Evan."

What?! All of a sudden, Steve seemed extremely interesting. He had insights into a human I wanted to know about— and we're not talking on the cellular level. He'd been mano a mano with one of my major crushes.

I acted casual.

"Oh yeah? You two good friends?"

"Not too close. We've just surfed together."

"What's he like?" I asked. *Am I really asking a date about another guy I like? I'm the worst.*

"He's really great, actually. But I don't really hang out with his crowd."

His "crowd"? *Please don't tell me Evan's some cliquey boy. I can't handle feeling like I'm in high school all over again.* "Oh," I said, "he has a crowd?"

"I don't know. Maybe. I guess I just don't really hang out with many crowds."

Right. I was out with *Steve. Must stop being nosey about Evan. I can do my research on other men on my own time.*

We walked into a dark room, and a black light came on, revealing glow-in-the-dark crystals tucked behind a glass case. In the light, they appeared dull, but in the dark, the rocks shined a bright lime green, a fiery red, and a mystical pale white.

I thought again about my attitude changes that had been happening over the last few weeks. They seemed small to me, but I figured if I looked at myself in the right way, with the right lighting, my tiny changes were actually much more vibrant than I'd thought. *I'm a glow-in-the-dark rock,* I thought, with goofy joy. *I shine.*

After our date, I narrowed my thirty dates down to my "favorites," which were around ten guys. And (luckily?) some of the guys had plans for Valentine's Day, which would make my decision about Date 31 easier. I used an online survey service to create my "Man Poll," listing the twenty-two men who said they'd be available for a Valentine's date with me on Saturday.

I figured I needed serious help making the decision. I mean, I have a hard enough time deciding what to eat for lunch every day. So how in the world was I to whittle down my list to just one guy, the grand pooh-bah of the evening?

That decision seemed to go well beyond my skill set.

This was it. I was surprisingly calm. And for the first time in more than a month, I sat at home alone on a Friday night. I'd become so accustomed to having an overly busy schedule that I wondered what life would be like postproject. Had I alienated my girlfriends, like some people do when they find a new boyfriend, and then they wonder if their friends will forgive them and spend time with them again after the breakup?

I called my girlfriends, sheepishly asking if they had plans. They did. I begged Rachel to ditch her party early, come hang out and watch the poll results until 3:00 AM, and then head to the television studios with me a couple hours later. It would be a long night, but a much-needed one.

I felt liberated, as if once again I could chat with my girlfriends all night. I called them all—Lumina, Cathy, Elena, Amy, Kat—and asked them to weigh in. Whom would they pick for me?

"I vote for you," said Rachel, as she sat on my couch, flipping through her gossip magazine.

"But who should I pick?"

"Well, who do you feel like picking? I know I'm usually all-knowing about everything, but this does happen to be your project."

"There are guys who I'd love to go out with, but they can't go. Allen—that guy I spilled my guts to at the comedy club—he's out of town for work. Kissy-face Nick is out of town for a wedding. And Tyler the D.C. doctor is in India, saving the world or something."

"Good. That narrows things down."

"I really liked Christian, the comedian who went to the Chinese New Year parade. And Dan, the young'un."

"I'm pretending I didn't just hear you say that."

"Juan-Carlos, the Catholic. And Derek, that guy I pretty much hated when I first met him? I like him, too."

"Okay . . ."

"But I'm kinda leaning toward two other guys more than any of them."

"And they are . . . ?"

"Jonathan, the dreamy guy."

"No surprise."

"And Evan, the guy who bailed me out last-minute."

"I figured."

We kept checking the numbers. Within the first few minutes, it looked like Jonathan would be the clear winner, raking in fifty-five of the first hundred votes. But the other guys quickly caught up, volleying for the top spot. With hundreds of people clicking on the survey, the leaders pulled ahead and battled for the top spot. Ryan pulled into the lead, then Derek handed it off to Paul, then to Evan. And then one name burst onto the scene, racking hundreds of points in an instant.

"Did Tyson totally just hijack the poll?" I asked, feeling my adrenaline kick in with curiosity. The same computer address kept appearing on the survey. Every three minutes, hundreds more votes for Tyson, my dumpling-run date, would post.

"I mean," Rachel assessed, "either he's in love with you or he just really wants to be on television."

Was that all he wanted from me? My television connections? The thought stung my Pollyanna heart. A few weeks before, I hadn't really cared why anyone agreed to go out with me; I had just needed to fill my calendar. But after meeting so many men and developing so many mini-crushes, I naively assumed none would go out of his way—even rig my cheesy poll—and use my risk-taking journey as a quick step into the limelight.

With my freshly adopted "let's be nice and give everyone the benefit of the doubt" attitude, I offered some options. "Maybe this isn't even from Tyson's computer. Maybe this is from, like, a roommate of his who really wants him to get out more. Or one of his old girlfriends, who wants him to win this date, figuring he'll be more marketable to other women." My twisted stomach relaxed a little.

"Who cares? He sucks," Rachel said. "I say you don't count his votes, and throw him out. He can be marketable using someone else's time."

If nothing else, I realized that I didn't mind not going on another date with Tyson. Even if his votes outweighed everyone else's a bazillion to one, he wasn't the guy I'd pick. I turned my focus back to the incoming numbers, and my stomach knots started to tangle again. No matter what the numbers showed, I'd still need to make a final decision.

"Since when did this whole project become so serious?" I asked. "It was just supposed to be fun and exciting. How did I end up caring so much about these guys? Or what our potential 'relationships' would look like?" I said with mocking finger quotes. How had this silly relationship recovery program that I'd created become so emotionally taxing?

I deleted all of Tyson's repeated votes just as three o'clock came and the final numbers trickled in. In all, around 1,500 *real* people had voted within six hours. The top choice ended up being Jonathan—who received 253 votes, barely sneaking by Evan, who received 241. Just a twelve-vote difference. And I still had no idea whom to choose.

I weighed my options.

"Both Evan and Jonathan would be fun to hang out with again," I said. "And I'd love to go out with both of them again, whether I pick them for tomorrow or not."

"Right," Rachel said.

"Which makes the decision difficult."

"It's just a decision," she said, shrugging and settling back into her magazine.

I sighed, trying to sink my thoughts deeper into my soul, somewhere near the spots where "reason" and "reality" lived. I tried to look into the future, to somehow sync my soul with the universe's intentions.

I recalled my dream date, walking along the beach at Coney Island. I remembered the feeling of my heart tripping as

Jonathan revealed every tidbit about himself, how he helped me save a dog, how he looked like a model for some fashion magazine. I tried to imagine our future, filled with dinner dates and parties with friends. He was social, probably liked to party. But what of substance? Did I see anything beyond the superficial? Could we be best friends as well as lovers?

"I could see myself dating him," I said, "and having a great time—lots of chemistry, for sure. Maybe even for a few months or so. But . . . eventually we'd probably see that our lifestyles were too different—him being more of a drinker, me going to Al-Anon and hanging out with Mormons. I just don't see that meshing in the long-run."

"But then there's Evan," I said, practicing the same forward-thinking pragmatism. He had been consistent over the past few weeks in contacting me—just enough to show me he was interested, but not so much as to seem pushy.

I remembered the connection I had felt with Evan, how calm and cool he was, and how he'd dropped his evening plans to rush to my rescue when Michael, the brainy medical student, couldn't make it to the play. And Evan made me laugh so easily! The thought made me smile and filled me with warmth. I loved how we'd chatted like old friends, and how I'd felt real around him, fully myself. I remembered the contours of his face, and the way he smiled openly, genuinely—nothing to hide. My gut swirled pleasurably at the memory of sitting beside him under the stars.

I inhaled deeply, wondering how to say what I felt. Dare I say the words out loud? "Evan . . . seems like the kind of guy I could marry."

Hearing myself say the word "marry" made me feel suddenly self-conscious, even foolish. What an outlandish prediction! And after only one date with him? I scolded myself, feeling stupid, and then Rachel interrupted my snowballing self-criticism.

"Well, there you go," she said, throwing her hands out, sounding satisfied.

I turned to see if she was rolling her eyes again. Nope. Just the blase "don't be surprised by my genius" look I've seen so often. Didn't my most crazy yet rational friend hear how ridiculous I sounded?

"Look," she said earnestly, as if clarifying a difficult equation, "these last thirty days have been great. They taught you all this stuff about life, and dating, and love, and blah, blah, blah," she said, waving her arms. "But, what's the other purpose of dating?"

I stared back blankly.

"To find your true love."

"Oh," I said, nodding my head, "right."

She nodded back at me. "Seriously, Tamara. If you think there's actually a chance of something with this guy, then go for it."

I called the television producers and spoke with doubt still trailing in my voice. "I think Evan might be the winner."

"You *think*?" said Eric, the producer on the other end.

"I'm pretty sure," I said, still uncertain.

"Well," he said, encouraging my certainty, "we need to figure out how to set up your segment. So either it's Evan or it's not."

What did I have to lose? In the scheme of life, and fate, and taking chances, perhaps this was the road I was meant to take all along. Maybe every date, every misstep, every insecurity and moment of second-guessing myself was one big template for today. If nothing else, I knew I'd have a great second date with him. And at that moment, that was good enough for me.

"Yes," I said. "It's Evan."

DATE 31
VALENTINE'S DAY:
THE SECOND DATE

Like most pivotal events in life, the day of my thirty-first date started early and rushed by as if the fast-forward button were stuck. I tried to focus on every little event, forcing myself to absorb every feeling of every moment, as if this could somehow slow time and stamp the details of the entire day permanently on my memory.

My day was a blur of new experiences. Like the moment the woman in hair and makeup brushed out my curls, making my hair look like a poofy fluffball. And the moment I sat on-air with the cast of *Good Morning America Weekend* and announced Evan as the winner.

"Do we have him on the phone?" asked Kate Snow.

I heard Evan's voice, sounding surprisingly bright for an early-morning phone call. "Hi," he said. He sounded different than I remembered from weeks ago. Maybe higher pitched.

"It's good to hear your voice," I said, trying to wrap my head around talking to Evan's disembodied voice, which boomed Oz-like through the studio.

"Yeah, you too," he said.

But are you anywhere as excited to hear my voice as I am to hear yours? I'd wanted to talk with Evan ever since our first date, but I'd limited my contact strictly to email, just as I had with everyone else.

My heart pounded and I tried to keep from blushing. I could feel my friends in the studio watching for my reaction. All eyes looming, hoping to read my thoughts. I tried to keep them to myself as best I could, looking as composed and cool as possible. After all, did I really want all of America to see me jumping for joy that I got to go out with him? Or any of the other guys who could be watching? I didn't want to hurt anyone's feelings. But let's be honest—I was totally stoked. Finally, I got the chance to hear Evan's voice again, even if we didn't get to say much to each other.

There was no time for small talk during my two minutes on-air. I announced my thirty-first date quickly; there were a few congratulations and well wishes and then I was expertly whisked offstage during a commercial break. After all that buildup, it felt anticlimactic. *That's it?* I still couldn't get over how different it was to work behind the camera instead of in front of it, which demanded a completely different form of concentration. But it went smoothly, and then it was off to the next taping.

Rachel had tagged along with me for the early morning media blitz and remained by my side as we hurried down the street to our next television pit stop, at Fox News. The makeup artist airbrushed my face with a gold spritzer. "This just brightens you up a little under the cameras," she said. I looked in the mirror, a little aghast, wondering how my orangey color would look framed by my poofy hair. I looked like an '80s country-music star. Denim dress, anyone? I looked to Rachel for support. "You look fine," she said. "Besides, it's just a few million people watching."

Gee, I feel so much better.

The producers led me onto the set, where the anchors sat juggling news, weather, and feature stories like mine. They met me briefly and seemed impressed by my tenacity.

The anchorwoman, flawless and composed, shared her own dating stats. "Thirty guys in a month? Wow. I remember feeling lucky if I got thirty first dates in *a year.*"

I thought back to my years of dating droughts, when I considered it a banner year if I'd gone out on *three* dates. No way was I feeling sorry for her.

"How'd you get thirty guys to go out with you?" she asked.

"I begged!" Everyone laughed.

But it was true. My friends had constantly come to my aid when it came to filling my calendar. I had relied on faith, too. On days that I freaked out about having empty slots, a calm inner voice had reminded me of that old *Field of Dreams* mantra, "If you build it, he will come."

This time I was all on my own—no cosmic phone call with Evan's voice booming from the heavens. It made me even more antsy to see him again, to hear his voice, to have that incredible feeling of just being next to him. I was just looking forward to seeing him again in the flesh.

Morning quickly turned to afternoon while Rachel and I rushed all over town as if this were an important mission: Project Valentine. Of course, it was anything but top secret.

We headed to Bloomingdale's on the East Side, where Rachel found a new dress for me on the sales rack. Shimmery, slimming, clearance. Perfect. I made phone calls to track down some Broadway tickets for the night, and finalized plans for dinner on the Upper West Side. I confirmed that the television crew knew to meet Evan and me at 6:30 PM. Everything was set.

Meanwhile, the other guys I'd gone out with sent me messages wishing me luck for the evening. Friends, too. Or some would ask, "What about Jonathan?"

Yes, what about Jonathan?

In all the hubbub, that question lingered, and there was a part of me that felt bittersweet sadness, as if I'd let somebody down. Did he like me as much as Evan did? Had I made the right choice?

Rachel and I headed to the salon. It felt good to get off my feet. I pushed away my cloud of uncertainty. I didn't want to perseverate; I didn't want to feel angst about it. Instead, I consciously set it aside, telling myself to just go with the moment, and relaxed into the comfy massage chair. We were treated to manicures and pedicures. I felt spoiled and famous. It was surreal.

"How nervous are you about all this?" Rachel asked.

"Completely," I said, and there it was again. I couldn't help it. "What if I made a mistake? What if Jonathan's feelings are hurt?"

"I'm sure he's fine," she said, rolling her eyes and relaxing into the chair.

I blew on my wet nails, considered what I was about to do, and did it anyway. I typed a quick text message to Jonathan, mentioning the votes had been nearly tied and the decision had been tough. "Can we meet up next week?" I wrote.

He quickly responded, "Sounds great!"

I sighed with relief. Everything was going to be fine. No fragile male egos had been harmed in my choosing. In fact, I seemed to be the only one who was feeling concerned about whether I'd made the right choice.

I turned to Rachel. "Do you think Evan knows I like him?"

"I think all of America now knows that you like him."

I had just enough time at home to get ready for the date, wash off my orange makeup, wash out my hairsprayed Dolly Parton hair, and try to tame my locks enough to look presentable. My mildly curly hair settled on a look that was a cross between shaggy dog and Albert Einstein. It would have to do.

The TV crew called, saying they were ready for my arrival. Evan had offered to pick me up at my apartment, but the producers wanted to capture our "reunion" shot at the restaurant. I felt bad that his chivalrous efforts had been thwarted. Instead, Evan waited patiently for me at the restaurant bar while the television crew made sure the lighting and sound were working well. Evan looked to all the world like he'd been stood up for Valentine's Day.

As the cab approached the restaurant, my hands started to shake. Had I made the right choice with Evan? Would we have fun? Would I regret this evening? Or count it as one of the highlights of my life?"

We pulled up to the restaurant, Ouest, and Evan was standing outside in a suit and tie, holding a bouquet of flowers. He looked even more handsome than I'd remembered. And happy. I could see his kind smile, even with the blinding television lights blocking most of my vision.

At that moment, my heart blossomed. *Evan . . . sweet, easygoing Evan.*

He walked to the car and opened the door, and our eyes caught for the first time in weeks. He suddenly felt so familiar to me that it seemed inconceivable this was only the second time in my life I'd been in his company. *Haven't I known you always?* my heart seemed to say.

"I'm so happy to see you!" I said, and it was truer than I ever would have expected. As he reached for my hand to help me out of the taxi, I felt my inner rhythm slow a little, taking in the moment. I felt calm, at peace, and yet totally giddy.

What should I do next? I wondered, suddenly feeling awkward, like a middle-schooler at her first dance. What I wanted to do was throw my arms around his neck and kiss him with joy, in welcome, but I didn't. We were "on," and I felt exposed and self-conscious. We hugged a little awkwardly, he with his free arm, and I felt the press of his hand on my back, pulling me close—reassuring, certain. Then he pulled away.

"It's really great to see you, too," he said, smiling. And then we both laughed, because this was silly—the whole scene. But I could tell by looking at him that he was up for the adventure. "Let's have fun," I whispered.

I didn't get any time to share much else before the audio guy, Dave, interrupted our reunion and offered to help put a microphone on me. "Does your dress unzip in the back?" he asked.

My attempts at modesty were pointless as my back flashed the rush of cars and people behind us on Broadway. Dave slipped the battery pack down my back and hooked it to my bra strap. As the crew checked my audio, I looked up into Evan's sweet blue eyes. "You look great," he said. I was filled with a rush of warm comfort remembering the feeling I had when I was around him the first time. His mere presence somehow assured me that everything would be okay.

I took a deep breath and tried to slow my racing heart, and just then Evan handed me the bouquet of flowers. "Happy Valentine's Day," he said. "There are thirty-one daisies."

I took them from him, grazing his fingers with mine, feeling an electric jolt as I did so. *I want to kiss you!* I thought. Instead, I held the flowers close to my chest.

"Did you take the time to count them all?" I teased.

"They're all there," he said, and I knew he was telling the truth—and that he probably had counted them!

"I have something for you, too, Evan." I reached into my pocket and pulled out a little box of candy conversation hearts. I handed them to him. "Thank you for being my Valentine." I meant it, even though I felt silly saying it.

He laughed. "I love these things!" He offered me his arm. "Shall we?" And he escorted me inside.

The crew followed behind us, and everyone in the restaurant watched us pass, no doubt wondering who we were. *Are they from a reality show? A sitcom? Who are they?* We certainly weren't the celebrities they'd hoped to see, but I felt like a star having the most surreal night of her life. After an entire month of meeting new people, questioning every thought and expression, and sometimes believing that I'd taken on a much bigger project than I could handle, I felt like we were celebrating a long journey's end.

Once we were settled at the table, I realized that everything we said was still being recorded. The spotlight shined down on us, the camera zoomed in close, and everyone in the restaurant watched. We could hardly say a word to each other, we were so stifled by the glare of lights and attention. I politely ordered the ravioli, and Evan ordered the snapper. Under such intense focus, it felt like we were speaking rehearsed lines from a movie. I'd never felt so exposed yet so giddy. I wanted to lean in and whisper like a kid, "Can you believe this!" But of course, I couldn't, so I said it with my eyes, and so did he. Our food came quickly, but when it did, he was also given ravioli. I pointed to the plate.

"Is that what you ordered?" I asked, prepared to call the waiter back.

"Yep," he said, and winked. No big deal. *What grace*, I thought, admiring him anew. Another man might have called the waiter to task, made a big stink of the mistake out of self-importance and arrogance. Not Evan. It's those small moments, I swear, that reveal a person's character. He was indeed the perfect choice for my thirty-first date. How had I ever had my doubts? And goodness, he was handsome. His watercolor eyes, his perfectly groomed face with a fresh shave, and his newly trimmed, dark brown locks of curly hair. He had even dressed up for our evening, in a tailored suit and a black tie.

"I like your suit," I said, reaching out to stroke his tie.

"Thanks," he said, smiling. "It's brand new."

"It is?" Had he spent the day preparing for our date, like I had?

"Of course it is," he said. "Tonight's a big deal. I had to make sure I tried to look half as good as you do. That dress is amazing. *You* look amazing."

And he was serious. No mention of my crazy hair. Just kind, sweet words.

Evan smiled as he dove into his ravioli. It was clear by his easygoing demeanor that he was just there to enjoy the evening. He seemed totally unaffected by the circus around us. I loved that about him. He didn't sweat the small stuff and didn't add drama to what was already a complicated situation. He was patient and genuinely did his best to enjoy every moment. Being around him helped calm me. He grounded me. His attitude was refreshing.

On our first date, there was a moment when I was sitting across from him, and I'd just broken off a corner of the cookie I was eating, listening to him talk, and I thought, *I could fall in love with this guy.* But he was only my sixth date into the project, so I resisted getting too attached so early on and kept my mind—and my options—open.

Still, we'd kept in touch. He was one of a few guys who'd checked in with me through email, asked how I was holding up, and showed interest and kindness. Our connection had deepened. I truly liked him as a person; I wasn't just attracted to his style and sensibilities. Not only that, but I respected him, too. These were essential qualities I hadn't weighed as heavily in my dating life before my project.

All of a sudden, we were once again interrupted. My friends from *Good Morning America Weekend,* anchors Kate Snow and Ron Claiborne, crashed our date. I knew they were coming, but Evan didn't. He smiled and welcomed them with firm handshakes, introducing himself, confident and totally at ease. They both slid into our booth, smiled warmly, and went into TV reporter mode, grilling Evan with questions: "What are your intentions with Tamara? How lucrative is your career? Are you a relationship guy or a player?"

Evan was a trouper as the interrogation was caught on camera, laughing and joking with Ron and Kate while pleading his case. "I think my career is pretty lucrative and secure. I work with marketing research. I mean, it's not like I majored in communications, right?" he teased. They loved him.

"You guys have a good night," Kate said on her way out. "We've got our own Valentine's celebrations."

"We'll see you tomorrow morning on the show, right?" asked Ron. I had almost forgotten that Evan and I had agreed to appear on the show in the morning. Was I really planning on wrapping up this project with a dramatic date just to turn around and get up in the wee hours to report everything to the world? How would I even be able to make sense of anything by then?

"We'll be there," I said.

After dinner, we caught a cab, left the camera crew behind, and went on our way to our next event, a surprise I'd cooked up for us.

It was such a relief to finally get Evan alone. "We can talk like normal people now," I said.

"You weren't really nervous, were you?" he asked. "You should be a pro with all that TV stuff by now."

"Are you kidding? Completely nervous." *But not because of those TV cameras, Evan. I'm nervous because I like you—duh.* "It's a big night," I said.

"It *is* a big night," he agreed, a huge smile lighting up his face. "Thank you for inviting me. I have to admit, I was really hoping I'd get to see you again tonight."

"You were?"

"I mean, I knew even if you didn't pick me for your thirty-first date that I'd want to see you again. But I'm glad it worked out this way," he said, looking at me softly.

I was still a little nervous in his presence, not totally accepting the reality that he was actually sitting next to me. As if I were in some crazy, amazing dream. I held his gaze with a shy smile. "I'm glad you wanted to come." I turned my head forward, blushing. "I can't wait until you see this show," I said.

"Can I guess what it is?" he asked, looking at me slyly.

"Sure, but you'll never guess," I teased.

"Is it *Billy Elliot?* I hear it's awesome."

"What! It is! How did you know? It was supposed to be a surprise." I gave him a playful sock in the arm. "You have no idea how glad I am you want to see it!"

We arrived at the Imperial Theatre and made our way to the fifth row—refreshingly free of media. It was fitting that since we'd connected over a theater date, we should revisit it tonight. Plus, theater enlivens me—in many ways, it's part of my makeup, and I wanted Evan to share that. I've been watching plays since I was a toddler, and I took acting and singing lessons as far back as I can remember. I dreamed of being a Broadway star, and theater was even one of my college majors. But for some reason, the stage and the audience resonated differently with me that night than it ever had before.

Usually there's a feeling of camaraderie among everyone in the theater. But it felt like more than that.

With Evan there, everything seemed to be in sync—seeing him catch my lingering glances out of the corner of my eye, feeling him at ease sitting close to me. It all seemed natural. Not intimidating. As if having him by my side was exactly where we belonged.

At one point, the show stopped and a voice came overhead. "Ladies and gentlemen, we need to take a quick break. There's an oil slick on the stage we need to clean up." I had never witnessed anything like that before. As the audience sat patiently, Evan reached into his coat pocket and opened the box of conversation hearts I had given him. He was looking for the cleverest one he could, despite the dimmed lights. "SWEET . . . LIPS . . . ?" he read, unsure.

He passed the candy heart to me just as the show picked back up. I eyed the writing closely and could barely hold in my laughter. "It says SWEETIE PIE," I corrected.

"I think I like 'sweet lips' better," he said, giving me a wink. Yes, I wondered about his sweet lips, too. We both stifled our laughter, drawing "Must you?" glances from people beside us. This was by far the best Valentine's Day I had ever had.

Sitting next to Evan, I felt calm, secure, and happy. Perhaps it was the spectacle of the evening, perhaps it was something more aligned with fate—whatever the case, I felt this entire project had a much grander purpose than I had ever expected. It felt somehow miraculous, as if this moment were meant to be. I looked away from the play and at Evan, eyeing the contours of his face as he responded to the action on the stage, unaware of my gaze. It felt so intimate to be doing such a small thing, and I realized then how vulnerable he was, too. Because I had pulled him along on this adventure—and not only was I putting my trust in him, but he was entrusting himself to me. I felt an overwhelming sense of loyalty and purpose and deep affection for him, startling myself with how profound it felt. *This is right*, I thought. I knew, right then, that Evan, my thirty-first date, would become so much more than just a media hook for Valentine's Day. Instead, I had no doubt tonight would change the trajectory of my life.

As I sat in the audience, I pondered what I'd learned about the difference between love and possession. In the past, I'd so desperately wanted someone to be mine. I had deeply coveted men's adoration. I had wanted to stamp my passport to Love-land and have the man be my souvenir, evidence that I had taken the journey. But what I needed most had little to do with men. It had to do with me. I knew now that I didn't need a man to "be mine," despite what the Valentine's candy says. What mattered was focusing more on being a loving person and actively striving to allow love in.

I didn't need a man. I didn't need a boyfriend. I needed to get over myself.

As the play came to a close, we stood for the ovation. I cheered not just for the show, but for every day—and every man—that I'd experienced over the last month. My journey was finally coming to an end, and I was finally making my exit.

It was late, and since we both had to get up early for our television interview, Evan and I headed toward the subway station. I was tired but content beside him. I didn't want to say goodbye. He took my hand; his felt warm and strong in mine. My heartbeat quickened, and I imagined him paddling through strong surf with those hands, typing up creative marketing strategies, touching me . . .

My fantasizing was suddenly disrupted by the night's most surreal moment: As we entered the subway station below Times Square, my many worlds collided.

Smack in the center of the station stood Tyson and his friends. That's right—Date 28 was standing in front of me. We both seemed startled with recognition and smiled. Then, out of the blue, Evan's roommate walked up, carrying a bag with some cheesecake. Before I could say hello to him—or Tyson—someone came up behind me and covered my eyes with her hands. I have no idea what made me guess her presence, but I knew immediately who it was.

"Kat?" I guessed. The hands gently gave way, and I turned around to see my photographer friend Kat, who had set me up with Jared, Date 7. I was speechless, trying to figure out if this was real or some sort of twisted episode of the Dating Project Twilight Zone. *Was this planned?* I wondered quickly. *Like a mini-flash mob?* Never before had I run into anyone I knew in the subway station at Times Square, much less a deluge of people linked to my dating world.

From behind me I heard someone scream, "Tamara!"

Now it was just getting weird. Okay, weird*er*. It was none other than my closest ally, Rachel, who had spent the entire day with me serving as my stylist and picking out every detail of my Valentine's Day wardrobe. I waited for someone to say, "Surprise!" But it was literal providence. There was no logic or planning behind this impossible cluster of people. They simply were all there at the same time. *Oh, Fate. You are mischievous.*

I turned to Evan with a curious look on my face. "Evan," I said, "This is all *real,* right?" He looked just as nonplussed as I did by it all.

Rachel sized up my date. "Evan, you're even cuter in person. Good job, Tam!" I was embarrassed. And elated.

There were rounds of introductions, a quick summary of the evening, and then everyone trickled away, heading to their own destinations. Evan and I stood and stared at each other for a few seconds, adjusting to what had just happened. I didn't want our night to end.

"I'm kinda craving that cheesecake my roommate was holding," he said suddenly, smiling slyly. "Do you want to go get some?"

I smiled and nodded.

We headed back outside into the busy streets. As thousands of others passed by, I felt as if I had just been witness to a little magic. I stood next to a man who had totally caught me by surprise. I hadn't expected to actually meet anyone I'd really like through my project—much less several men, or one who wasn't even meant to be part of the project to begin with—and yet here we were . . . Coincidence or fate? How could I not see it as the latter?

While I'd made all my plans, what I hadn't expected was that the *un*expected would be even better than I'd hoped. I'd started out this project as a cynic, thinking there were "no good guys in New York." But I just hadn't been looking hard enough. Only when I had stepped away from the plans, let myself go a little, and loved a little more, had I been able to see the good parts of people. As it turned out, the best parts weren't part of my plan at all.

I stopped walking suddenly. Cars and people rushed past us. This time, I didn't care.

"Evan?"

He looked at me. He understood. Without a word, he took me in his arms, and for the first time, I felt the lips of somebody I knew I could love—*without* needing to be loved back.

He pulled away slowly, and said, his voice low, "I told you so."

I looked at him quizzically, blushing in spite of myself.

"Sweet lips . . . " he whispered.

I laughed and kissed him again. Just to prove him right.

EPILOGUE

Seven months after the project, I stood on that same subway train that had once been host to my public display of heartbreak. The doors opened and a group of passengers squeezed by. A familiar voice muttered a soft "excuse me" as he bumped past me and weaved his way to an empty seat. I recognized his familiar figure instantly and stared at his reflection in the subway window. His light brown hair was perfectly messed, and he wore a puffy vest with a flannel shirt, a combination only he could pull off as "cool." His hazel eyes burrowed into the copy of *The New Yorker* he sat reading, just as he had appeared when I first met him on Date 27.

He still made me weak in the knees.

Even months later, he had an alluring power. He was a mystery to me, a mixture of brilliance and boyish charm. And I could think of nothing more than the moment we'd parted and how desperately I had wanted to kiss him that day.

We had talked about meeting up again, but I knew he'd be one of the many guys who would drift away and remain in the realm of "acquaintance." Could things have actually gone differently? Could he ever have been anything more?

What should I say?

As I rehearsed my cool introduction in my head, all I could think about were the words I truly wanted to tell him but was too scared to say. I thought of pouring out my soul to him. Admitting every thought and desire he conjured in my mind. Telling him how he made my heart dance during our brief encounter. To me, he was more than just another man who spent one day with a girl on a date. He was among the many good men who formed a gracious and alluring backdrop against which I learned so much about myself—namely, that self-worth, identity, and fulfillment don't come in a package labeled "boyfriend" or "husband"—it comes from within. True intimacy, friendship, and love will follow. It was in my reach, no matter who I was with.

Love was something to offer, not to seek. And it now seemed more alive within me and everyone around me. I learned to look at the world a little differently through each of these men. I opened up, corralled judgment, and let myself be me among them—for my own sake, not theirs. Their acceptance and respect in return reinforced my sense of self rather than defined it. Very simply, I grew. I traded disillusionment for hope.

I wanted to tell him all of the important lessons I'd learned. I wanted him to know how thankful I was that he existed in the world. I wanted him to know that our few hours together played a role in who I was becoming.

The train stopped. As the doors opened and we both made our exit, I hesitated, then reached out and put my hand on his shoulder. He turned.

"Hi, Nick."

He shook his head slightly in surprise, trying to pinpoint how he knew me. "Hi," he said slowly, a sign of recognition rising in his eyes. Then his face broke into a large friendly smile as he realized it was me. "Hi!" he said again. "How are you? I saw you on TV. How's all that going?"

I gave him a brief update on my life and let him know how much I appreciated his help. He thanked me back, and I realized then that many of these men likely also had something to learn, or were still learning, and that perhaps I, too, had made a positive impact on their perspectives about dating— and women.

We stood in the train station, having run out of things to say. But it was comfortable.

"We'll have to catch up sometime. Meet up for coffee?" he said, turning to go.

"I'd love to," I said, smiling, but I knew that neither of us would follow up on the invitation. And that was fine. I'd said all that I wanted.

As I walked up the stairs and crossed the street, I was overwhelmed by a rush of remembering everything I had gone through. After thirty-one days of dating, I had changed my attitude on life and love. I had challenged myself to face my fears, and by default, I had become my best self. I had changed. I had retired from my relationship retirement. I had hope. And I was happy.

A smile lit up my face as I saw Evan waiting for me on the corner. He was still my companion, my teacher and friend, and over the months he had grown into something more. My dating project had taught me to date differently, to relax and allow true love into my heart. I had finally learned how to appreciate each date as a joyous experience, without expectation. And somewhere along the way—after our one hundredth date or so—we fell in love.

Evan reached for my hand, recently adorned with a ring, and smiled.

"You ready to go explore more of the city?" he asked.

"You bet," I said.

I'm ready for anything.

ACKNOWLEDGMENTS

First, my biggest thanks to Merrik Bush-Pirkle, my editor at Seal Press. She helped translate my Sanskrit, thoroughly answered my nosy curiosities and concerns, cheered for me when doubt crept in, and made my first book-writing experience more blissful than I could have dreamed. You have an incredible gift. Thank you for sharing it with me.

To my agent, Frank Weimann, of The Literary Group International, thank you for seeing a tiny article about my engagement and envisioning my story as something bigger. And to his assistant, Elyse Tanzillo, for always keeping my confidence afloat and reminding me there's no other shoe to drop.

Thanks also to Brooke Warner, executive editor at Seal Press, for your confidence in my book, for your vision, and for taking on a first-time author.

Many of those who've supported me through my dating project and through the writing of my book are my girlfriends, those dear souls who always seem to get me through the joys and journeys in my life. To my girls who helped me along the way, thank you for listening to me and being willing to chat about my book: Anna Song Canzano, Amber Stahr Bristow, Lumina Gershfield, Kat Hennessey, Marcia Chaney, Sarah Lemblé, Allison Anslinger, Elena Genovese, Megan Shirk, Mitzi Flade Sampson, Kelly Paluso, Jessica Bean, Felice Austin, and the Wednesday night writing girls.

Rachel Smith, thank you for making me look good, for staying up into the wee hours, and for being real.

Amy Middleton, thank you for suggesting I be proactive in my dating life and turn my misery into mastery. Thank you for all the foundations you helped me lay with my project, my website, and my book.

My very first friend, my constant, Catherine Kiefer Branch, thank you for always being there for me, for listening to me complain about every boy I've ever liked, and for constantly celebrating my very existence.

Mom, you always say the right thing at the right time. Thanks for knowing I will never give up on anything and for having the wisdom not to tell me such. And thank you to my awesome family for loving me and tolerating my absence as I scurried away into a corner to write. You're so patient!

To all those who found me dates, thank you for making my project your priority. I couldn't have made it without your constant help with filling my calendar with quality men. Thank you, Katie Baker, Mary Taylor, Catherine Branch, Mike Matthews, Kellie Rentz, Lumina Gershfield, Kat Hennessey, Brandon Lisy, Brooke and Nathan Schmoe, Megan Perkins Parker, Elena Genovese, Amber Stahr Bristow, Rachel Smith,

Stephanie Matsumura and Joel Beal, Jessica Roberts, and Vanessa Sparling.

Thank you to life and relationship coach Val Baldwin for all your help over the years and your constant stream of support.

Thank you to every guy I've crushed on, dated, been rejected by, fallen in love with, thought my life would end if I didn't marry. And to those guys who somehow found your way into those little corners of my heart, thank you for all that you've taught me, no matter the risk or the struggle.

And, of course, thank you to the thirty men who have forever changed my life. You each have helped teach me how to love better and to live fully. And thank you for your continued friendship and support. I'm forever grateful.

I'm especially thankful for my sweet, loving husband, who is more patient, kind, and funny than I could ever hope to be. Thank you for your willingness to be part of my project, for marrying me, for constantly listening to me talk about a couple dozen other guys I went out with one month, and for listening to me gripe all too often. You deserve a medal. Thank you for accepting my love as a consolation prize.

And to those of you who have read this book or my blog, thank you for being part of the journey.

ABOUT
THE AUTHOR

Tamara Duricka Johnson is a journalist, blogger, and freelance writer with a background in television news. She was a writer for ABC's *Good Morning America* and has been a newscast producer at KATU-TV in Portland, Oregon; KSL-TV in Salt Lake City, Utah; and WSLS-TV in Roanoke, Virginia. She is a member of the Writers Guild of America.

A proud Roanoke College alumna, she received her master of arts degree from Columbia University's Graduate School of Journalism, where she was awarded the Lee Bollinger Fellowship. It was in grad school that Tamara first started writing about dating in New York, when she examined the dating lives of single Mormons in Manhattan and created her master's project, a radio documentary called *Celibacy and the City*.

Tamara is an avid movie-and theatergoer who is obsessed with hot chocolate, has a love/hate relationship with running, and is constantly in search of the world's best spicy tuna roll. She lives in Los Angeles with her husband.

SELECTED TITLES FROM SEAL PRESS

  For more than thirty years, Seal Press has published groundbreaking books. By women. For women.

A Year Straight: Confessions of a Boy-Crazy Lesbian Beauty Queen, by Elena Azzoni. $17.00, 978-1-58005-361-7. A hilarious memoir documenting what happened when a lesbian beauty queen suddenly decided she wanted to start dating men.

The Choice Effect: Love and Commitment in an Age of Too Many Options, by Amalia McGibbon, Lara Vogel, and Claire A. Williams. $16.95, 978-1-58005-293-1. Three young, successful, and ambitious women provide insight into the quarterlife angst that surrounds dating and relationships and examine why more options equals less commitment for today's twentysomethings.

Just Don't Call Me Ma'am: How I Ditched the South for the Big City, Forgot My Manners, and Managed to Survive My Twenties with (Most of) My Dignity Still Intact, by Anna Mitchael. $15.95, 978-1-58005-316-7. In this disarmingly funny tale about the choices that add up to be her twentysomething life, Anna Mitchael offers young women comic relief—with the reality check that there's no possible way to hit all of their desired benchmarks on the way to thirty.

Kissing Outside the Lines: A True Story of Love and Race and Happily Ever After, by Diane Farr. $24.95, 978-1-58005-390-7. Actress and columnist Diane Farr's unapologetic, and often hilarious, look at the complexities of interracial/ethnic/religious/what-have-you love.

Follow My Lead: What Training My Dogs Taught Me about Life, Love, and Happiness, by Carol Quinn. $17.00, 978-1-58005-370-9. Unhappy with her failing love affair, her stagnant career, and even herself, Carol Quinn enrolls her two Rhodesian ridgebacks in dog agility training—and becomes the "alpha dog" of her own life in the process.

Second Wind: One Woman's Midlife Quest to Run Seven Marathons on Seven Continents, by Cami Ostman. $16.95, 978-1-58005-307-5. The story of an unlikely athlete and an unlikely heroine: Cami Ostman, a woman edging toward midlife who decides to take on the challenge to run seven marathons on seven continents—and finds herself in the process.

Find Seal Press Online
www.SealPress.com
www.Facebook.com/SealPress
Twitter: @SealPress